CUBE
BOOK

CUBE
BOOK

CARS

WHITE STAR PUBLISHERS

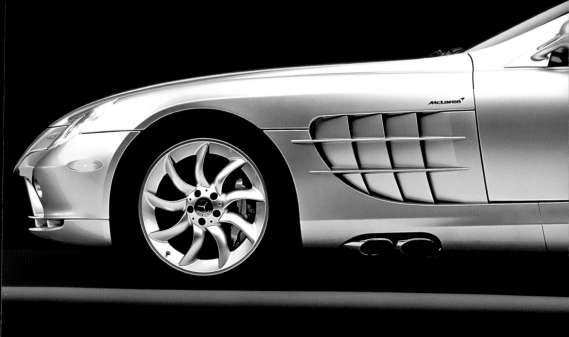

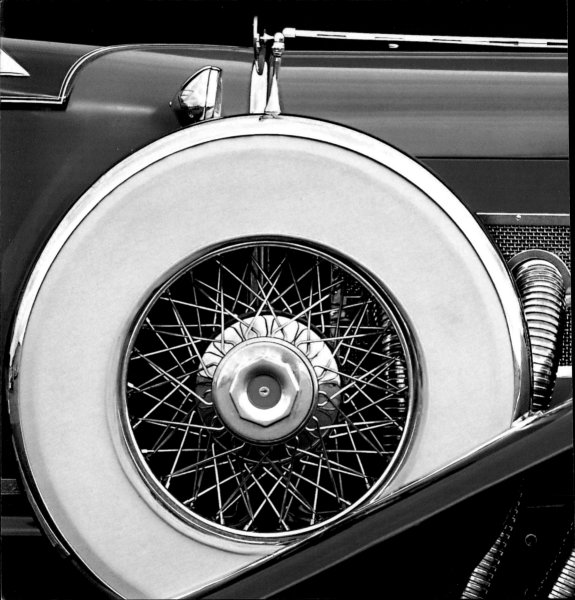

EDITED BY

VALERIA MANFERTO DE FABIANIS

text by
ENZO RIZZO

graphic design
CLARA ZANOTTI

graphic layout
MARIA CUCCHI

editorial staff
LAURA ACCOMAZZO
GIADA FRANCIA

translation
SARAH PONTING

© **2006 WHITE STAR S.P.A.**
VIA CANDIDO SASSONE, 22-24
13100 VERCELLI - ITALY
WWW.WHITESTAR.IT

• The Ferrari 250 GT by Pininfarina.

ISBN-13: 978-88-544-0172-3

REPRINTS:

3 4 5 6   11 10 09 08 07
Printed in Singapore
Color separation: Chiaroscuro, Turin, Italy

CONTENTS

CARS

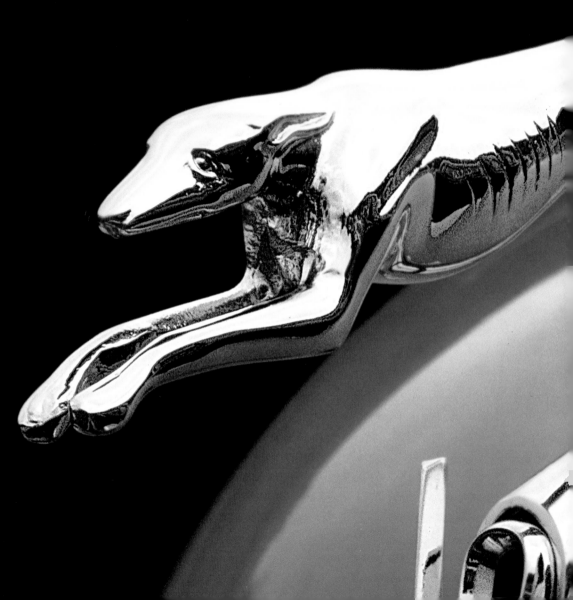

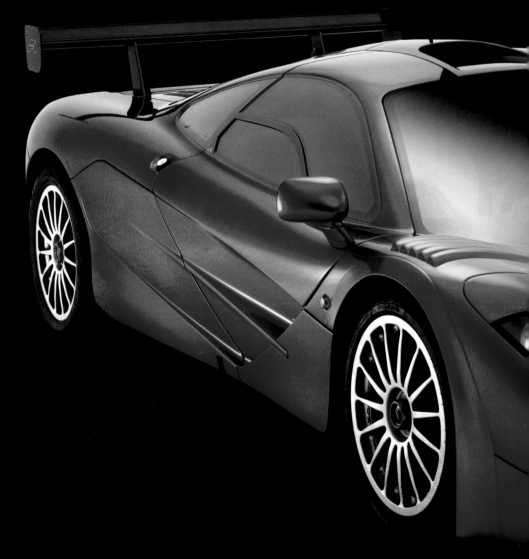

Introduction

THE COMMON DENOMINATOR OF THIS BOOK IS THE CUBE: ON THE ONE HAND IT IS THE GEOMETRIC SHAPE THAT INSPIRES THE PARTICULAR FORMAT OF THIS BOOK, WHILE ON THE OTHER IT IS THE UNIT OF MEASUREMENT – CUBIC CENTIMETER – OF THE ENGINE, THE VERY ESSENCE OF THE CAR. AND INDEED, THE CAR DISPLAYS A GREAT NUMBER OF ESSENCES, EACH WITH ITS OWN IDENTITY, BUT CONNECTED TO ALL THE OTHERS. TOGETHER THEY ARE CAPABLE OF TRACING THE HISTORY OF ONE OF MAN'S MOST REVOLUTIONARY INVENTIONS, FROM THE BEGINNINGS TO THE PRESENT DAY, FOR THE CAR IS THE CREATION THAT MORE THAN ANY OTHER REFLECTS MAN'S STATES OF MIND, NEEDS, AND

● The strips of the 1932 Auburn Boattail Speedster's radiator grille are the same color as the bodywork.

Introduction

DEVELOPMENT. CREATED AS A MEANS OF TRANSPORT AT THE END OF THE NINETEENTH CENTURY, THE CAR HAS REFINED ITS DURABILITY AND RELIABILITY, REACHING AND EVEN EXCEEDING ITS LIMITS.

IT HAS DEMANDED EXCLUSIVE STAGES, BECOMING A SPECTACLE CAPABLE OF DRAWING AN AUDIENCE AND THUS CONCENTRATING THE INTEREST OF THE MASSES UPON ITSELF, MULTIPLYING SALES OF ROAD MODELS. DURING ITS DEVELOPMENT IT HAS BECOME INCREASINGLY BEAUTIFUL, COMPLETE, LUXURIOUS, SAFE, AND ECO-FRIENDLY. THE PAGES OF THIS BOOK PORTRAY THE VARIOUS ESSENCES OF THE CAR, ILLUSTRATED BY PICTURES MORE THAN WORDS, LIKE A SEQUENCE OF

Introduction

FRAMES OF A FILM THAT TELLS AN UNFINISHED STORY, ONE THAT IS INCREASINGLY DESTINED TO CONSTITUTE A MODEL TESTIMONY TO MAN'S CAPACITY FOR EVOLUTION AND INNOVATION.

EACH OF THE CHAPTERS OFFERS THE READER A DIFFERENT VIEWPOINT OF THE CAR, FROM THE MOST ORIGINAL PROTOTYPES (CONCEPT CARS) TO RACING, BOTH ON THE ROAD AND ON THE TRACK; FROM THE MODELS THAT EPITOMIZE LUXURY TO THOSE THAT SEEK BEAUTY AND BECOME WORKS TO EXHIBIT; FROM THE UNFORGETTABLE CARS CREATED BEFORE WORLD WAR II, AND WHICH CHANGED THE COURSE OF HISTORY, TO THE RUNABOUTS THAT HAVE CONQUERED THE MAR-

Introduction

KET, BECOMING MASS PHENOMENA, AND THE MODELS THAT HAVE IRREVERSIBLY LINKED THEIR DESTINY TO A LOGO, EMBLEM, OR SYMBOL.

IN SHORT, THIS BOOK IS A JOURNEY IN WHICH THE UNDISPUTED STAR IS THE CAR. MAN'S PRESENCE CAN BE SENSED BEHIND THE SCENES, BECAUSE AN IDEA AND A DESIGN UNDERLIE EACH AND EVERY MODEL. HOWEVER, FOR ONCE THE LIMELIGHT IS ON THE CAR ALONE, VIEWED IN ITS ENTIRETY AND DETAILS, AS BEAU-TIFUL AS A SCULPTURE, A MASTERPIECE OF TECHNOL-OGY AND ART.

29 ● The 1932 Imperial features a gazelle on the hood.

30 to 39 ● The 1936 Mercedes 540K Cabriolet; the 1998 New Beetle; the 1963 Aston Martin DB5; the 1987 Ferrari F40; the tail of the 1954 Alfa Romeo Bat 5.

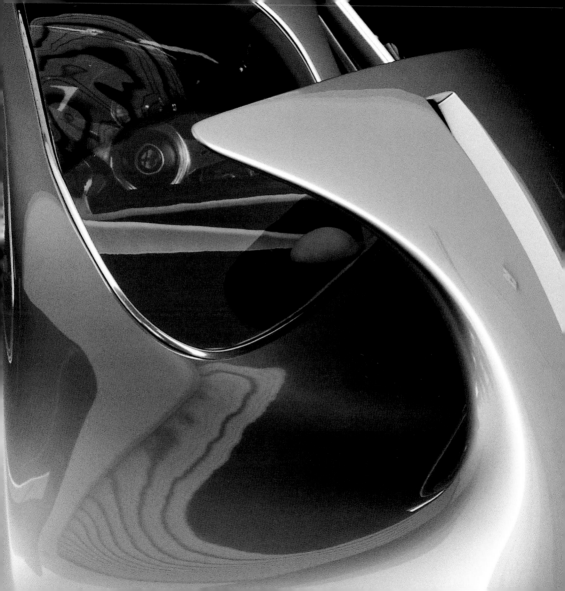

GRAND
DAMES

• The 1937 Mercedes 770K is characterized by an elegant chrome radiator.

INTRODUCTION Grand Dames

ALTHOUGH THE CAR HAS NOT YET CELEBRATED ITS FIRST CENTENARY, IT HAS ALREADY HAD TO FACE TWO WORLD WARS AND A SERIOUS ECONOMIC CRISIS. NONETHELESS, BETWEEN THE GREAT DEPRESSION OF 1929 AND WORLD WAR II, THE MOTOR INDUSTRY PRODUCED LUXURIOUS AND EXTREMELY BEAUTIFUL MODELS. DURING THE 1920S A "MASS MOTORIZATION" DRIVE HAD COMMENCED THAT REQUIRED PRACTICAL BUT NOT NECESSARILY HANDSOME VEHICLES. HOWEVER, DURING THE THIRTIES – PERHAPS TO EXORCIZE THE NARROW ESCAPE FROM POVERTY – CAR DESIGNS BECAME EXCEPTIONALLY ELEGANT, DUE TO THE ESTABLISHMENT OF STYLE CENTERS BY THE LEADING MOTOR MANUFACTURERS. THIS PERIOD WITNESSED A BOOM OF WORKSHOPS THAT

INTRODUCTION Grand Dames

STITCHED THE BODY STRUCTURE AND FITTINGS TO THE BARE CHASSIS WITH TAILOR-LIKE SKILL. AUTHENTIC WORKS OF ART THAT ARE STILL CONTEMPLATED WITH WONDER TODAY TESTIFY TO THIS AGE OF FERMENT IN EUROPE AND ACROSS THE ATLANTIC. THESE MARVELS WERE OFFSPRING OF TIMELESS TASTE AND EXTRAORDI-NARY TECHNOLOGICAL DEVELOPMENTS. THEY EMBOD-IED THE PASSAGE TO MONOCOQUE BODIES THAT INCOR-PORATED THE FENDERS TO GIVE RISE TO MODERN-LOOKING CARS, WHICH WERE NO LONGER RELATIVES OF CARRIAGES. IN EUROPE THE LEADING REPRESENTATIVES OF THIS FOUR-WHEELED BEAUTY AND LUXURY MOVE-MENT WERE MERCEDES AND ROLLS-ROYCE, WITH MAIN-LY CABRIOLET MODELS, WHICH COMBINED REFINED IN-

Grand Dames

Introduction

TERIORS WITH ELEGANT LINES, SUCH AS THE MERCEDES 540K, BUILT IN 1936 – THE LAST STAR TO SHINE BEFORE THE WAR. THE GERMAN MANUFACTURER ALSO COMPOSED OTHER HYMNS TO BEAUTY, SUCH AS THE SSK AND THE S680, THE LATTER WITH THE DECISIVE TECHNICAL CONTRIBUTION OF FERDINAND PORSCHE. THEN THERE WERE THE ROLLS-ROYCES, SPORTS CARS SUCH AS THE ALFA ROMEO 6C GRAN SPORT, AND – ACROSS THE ATLANTIC – MASTERPIECES SUCH AS THOSE MANUFACTURED BY DUESENBERG AND CORD.

THE FOLLOWING PAGES OFFER EVOCATIVE PORTRAITS OF THE MOST ALLURING "GRAND DAMES" IN MOTORING HISTORY.

- The Mercedes 540K Cabriolet (1936–1942) has a rounded tail and tiny lights.

46 • The first mass-produced car, the 1911 Ford Model T, was only available in black.

46-47 • The Ford Model T acquired a second row of seats and a certain elegance in 1919.

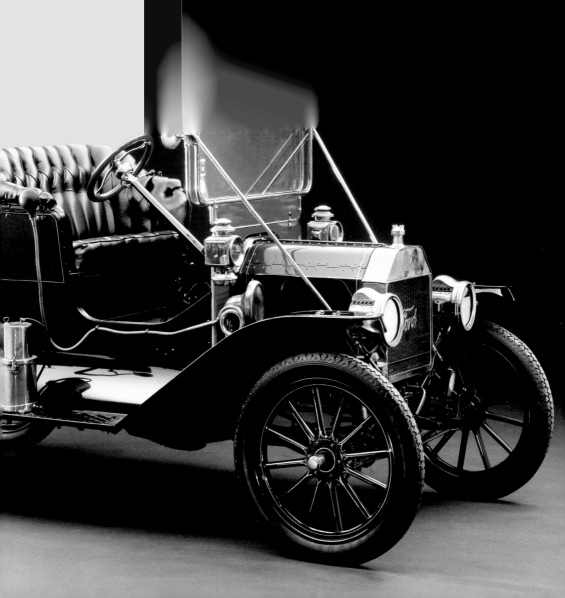

This 1903 Cadillac Model A Runabout is characterized by an elegant cardinal red color.

Red again, but the sides of the wheels and the roof of the 1923 Duesenberg Model A are light colored.

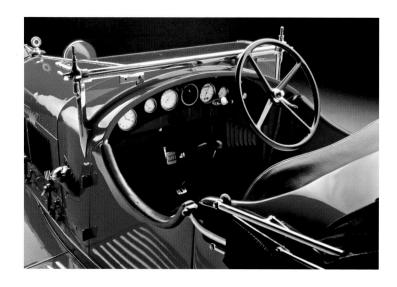

52 • The elegant interior of the Alfa Romeo 6C 1750 Gran Sport (1930-1932).

53 • The sporty 8-cylinder Alfa Romeo 8C 2300 has an elegant nose.

54-55 • The Isotta Fraschini Type 8 (1919-1935) features an open driver's seat and an extra long-range headlamp.

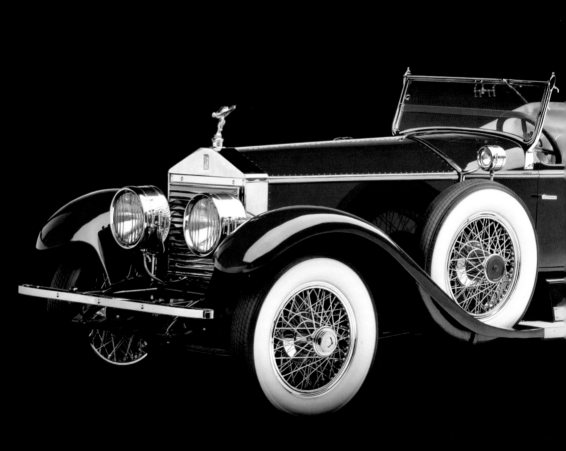

56-57 • Rolls-Royce does not just mean limousines: this photograph shows the sleek 1925 Rolls-Royce Piccadilly Roadster.

58-59 • The color of this 1928 Cadillac 34IA Dual Cowl Sport Phaeton is both bright and elegant.

The side view of this Rolls-Royce Silver Ghost clearly illustrates how the car is descended from the carriage.

62 • While imposing, this late-1920s Mercedes S680 has just two seats, like all authentic roadsters.

63 • The nose of the Mercedes S680: note the pointed radiator grille with the two emblems on the sides and a third above the radiator.

64-65 • No costs were spared on the wood and leather for the interior of the Mercedes S680 (1926-1930).

66 • The top of the 1930 Cord Torpedo L-29 is the same shade of white as the sides of the wheels, including the spare one.

67 • The nose of the Cord Torpedo L-29: the top extends to cover the front seats as well.

68-69 • The 1935 Duesenberg SJ features a double windshield and a cylinder grille.

70-71 • This two-tone 1932 Bugatti 50 Coupe is sleek, sporty, and elegant.

• Duesenberg also
chose the combination
of red and blue for the
1930 Model J Torpedo.

74-75 • The design of this 1930 two-tone La Salle Roadster is simply splendid.

76-77 • The proportions of the nose and tail of this 1932 Stutz DV-32 Convertible are practically identical.

78 and 79 • Variations on the theme of two-tone bodywork: an alluring 1932
Auburn Boattail Speedster.

80-81 • This early-1930s Auburn Boattail Speedster has a noble bearing and endless class.

The black bodywork of this 1932 Chrysler Imperial is highlighted with red details.

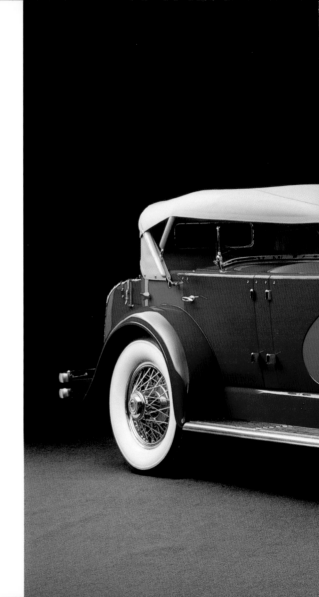

84 ● The tail of this 1935 Duesenberg SJ features a car trunk in the same color as the bodywork.

84-85 ● The covered version of the 1935 Duesenberg SJ retained all the elegance of the open model.

86-87 ● This 1933 Rolls-Royce is all black and chrome, revealing its exclusiveness at a glance.

● While sporty in style, this 1933 Jaguar Sport Tourer had four seats and pronounced running boards.

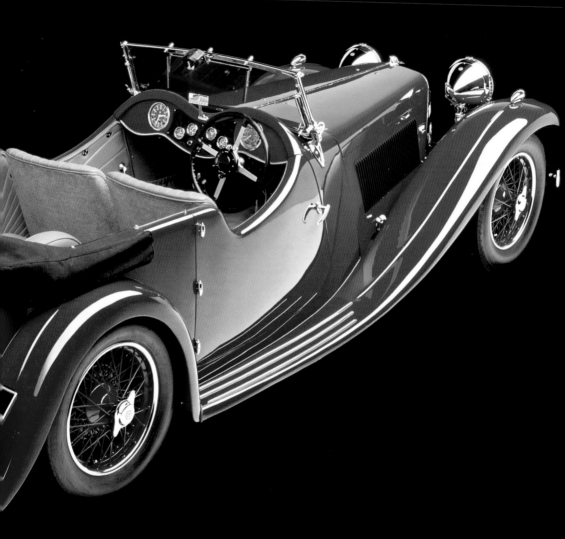

90 and 91 • Although it resembles a carriage, the innovative feature of the 1936 Chrysler Airflow is represented by the fenders and built-in lights.

92-93 • This 1935 Bugatti Type 57 has two-tone bodywork.

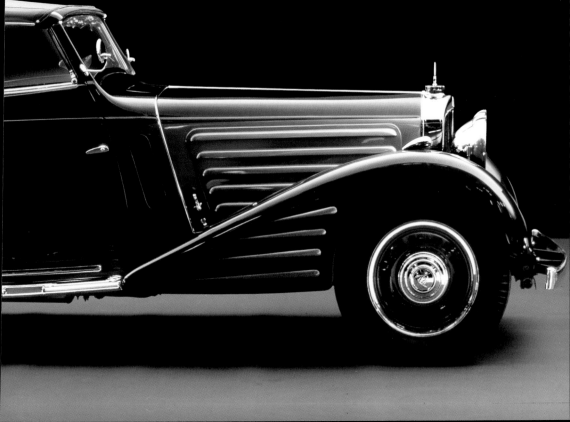

94-95 ● The rounded tail of the 1936 Maybach Zeppelin V12 was surprising for the period.

96-97 ● This sporty-looking 1937 Lagonda Rapide boasts few cosmetic frills and a delicate color.

98-99 ● This 1937 Bentley features an unusual, but very successful, combination of colors.

100-101 ● Bright red for a sports car, unusual for a Mercedes: in this case a 1936 Convertible.

102 • The 1934 Citroën Traction Avant triggered the monocoque revolution.

103 • The nose of the 1934 Citroën Traction Avant features a huge emblem
on the radiator grille.

104, 105 and 106-107 • Blue is France's racing color, sported here by a Talbot Lago T150 SS with black fenders.

108-109 • This 1937 Alfa Romeo 8C 2900B Spider boasts both class and well-balanced forms.

110 • The 1936 Alfa Romeo 8C 2900 is characterized by a long nose that houses the
eight-cylinder engine.

111 • The rounded tail with central lights of the 1936 Alfa Romeo 8C 2900.

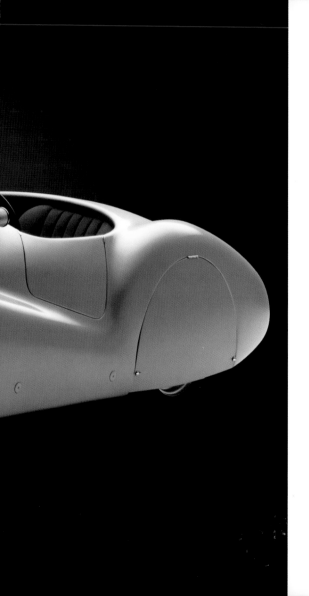

112-113 • This sporty 1940 BMW
328 is sinuous and seductive
in its silver livery.

113 • With its streamlined
fenders, the tail of the BMW 328 is
devoted to achieving excellent
aerodynamics.

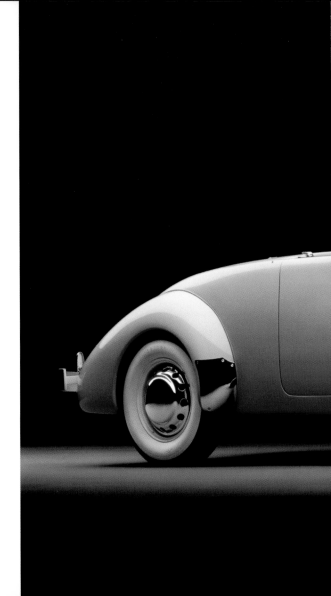

- The 1936 Cord 810 boasts an imposing totem-like nose with square hood.

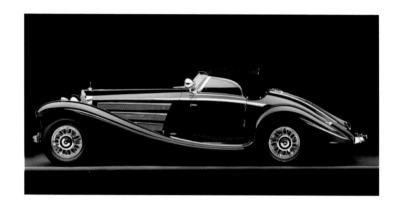

116 • The long hood was designed to house the Mercedes 540K Cabriolet's eight-cylinder 5400 cc engine.

117 • A detail of the chrome parts and exhausts of the Mercedes 540K Cabriolet.

118 and 119 • This 1938 Lincoln with built-in radiator grille is the Zephyr.

120-121 • The Ford Lincoln Continental features a two-tone hardtop and unusual porthole window.

122-123 • The 1947 Bentley MK VI is distinguished by streamlined two-tone fenders with built-in running boards.

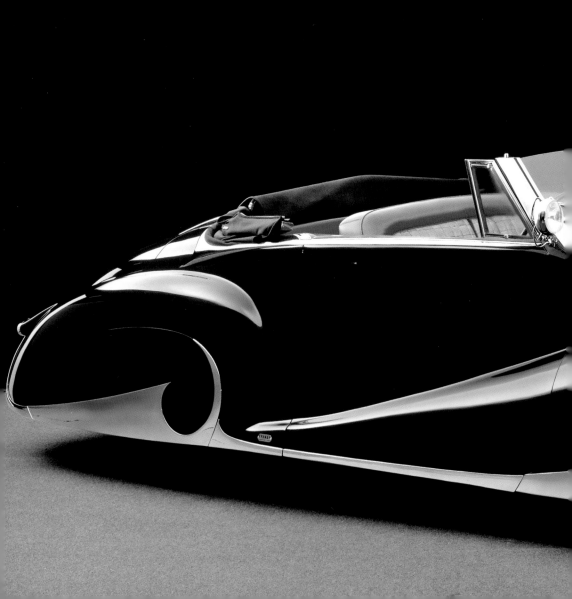

FAMILY EMBLEMS

• Rolls-Royces have always been distinguished by the "Spirit of Ecstasy" mascot, as displayed on this 1925 model.

INTRODUCTION Family Emblems

OF COURSE, THERE'S THE NAME BUT IT'S THE EMBLEM THAT IS THE REAL SYMBOL OF A CAR, THE DISTINCTIVE MARK THAT IDENTIFIES IT AND THE BADGE THAT TESTIFIES TO ITS NOBLE LINEAGE OR MORE HUMBLE ORIGINS. SHIELDS, INITIALS, AND SLOGANS ARE JOINED BY THE NEVER-FORGOTTEN MASCOTS THAT ONCE ADORNED RADIATOR CAPS – LUCKY CHARMS DEVISED TO PROTECT THE CAR AND ITS PASSENGERS. THESE MASCOTS WERE INSPIRED BY WORKS OF ART ORIGINALLY DESIGNED FOR GENTLEMEN'S HOMES AND DISTINGUISHED THE CARS PRODUCED DURING THE FIRST HALF OF THE TWENTIETH CENTURY. TODAY, FIFTY YEARS ON, THEY HAVE BECOME A RARITY AND SURVIVE ONLY IN THE FORM OF THE THREE-POINTED MER-

INTRODUCTION Family Emblems

CEDES STAR, DESIGNED BY DAIMLER, AND THE ROLL-ROYCE "SPIRIT OF ECSTASY," CREATED BY THE FAMOUS ARTIST AND SCULPTOR CHARLES SYKES. THERE ARE EMBLEMS TO SUIT ALL TASTES: THE MASERATI TRIDENT, THE FERRARI PRANCING HORSE, DESIGNED BY FRANCESCO BARACCA, AND THE PORSCHE RAMPANT HORSE (THE SYMBOL OF THE CITY OF STUTTGART), THE BMW STYLIZED PROPELLER, AND THE CITROËN DOUBLE CHEVRON, WITHOUT FORGETTING THE EXAMPLES FROM THE ANIMAL KINGDOM, SUCH AS JAGUARS (JAGUAR), LIONS (PEUGEOT), HORSES (MUSTANG), SNAKES (ALFA ROMEO), AND EVEN ELEGANT STORKS ABOUT TO TAKE FLIGHT, LIKE THE HISPANO SUIZA MASCOT.

Family Emblems

Introduction

THE RADIATOR CAPS OF YESTERDAY AND THE GRILLES OF TODAY RECOUNT THE HISTORY OF THE CAR, ITS DEVELOPMENT, AND ITS LEADING PLAYERS AS THOUGH THEY WERE BOOKS. CITROËN, PEUGEOT, ROLLS-ROYCE, FERRARI, PORSCHE, LANCIA, CHRYSLER, DAIMLER, BUGATTI, AND BENTLEY ARE NOT SIMPLY NAMES, BUT MEN AND FATHERS OF OUR WORLD – WITHOUT FORGETTING THEIR JAPANESE COUNTERPARTS, SUCH AS HONDA AND TOYOTA. THE LATTER HAVE CHOSEN EMBLEMS USING INTERSECTING LINES OR GEOMETRIC SHAPES, SUCH AS THE TOYOTA ECLIPSES AND THE MITSUBISHI DIAMONDS, ALONG WITH SOME RATHER EXOTIC DESIGNS SUCH AS SUBARU'S CONSTELLATION OF THE PLEIADES.

- The nose of the Alfa Romeo Giulietta Sprint, produced between 1954 and 1965, was characterized by the chrome shield.

130 ● The Fiat logo on the blue ground of this 1913 Tipo Zero has been revived for the models of the third millennium.

131 ● The Ford "signature" on the first mass-produced car, the Model T, in this case the 1911 version.

132 • A stylized bird adorned the radiator grille of the 1931 Studebaker President.

133 • An elegant stork embellishes the radiator cap of the 1922 Hispano Suiza H6B
Labourdette Skiff Torpedo.

134 • The badge of this 1930s Duesenberg features the outline of a female figure.

135 • The Duesenberg emblem, shown here on a 1923 Straight 8 touring, was inspired by a flying eagle.

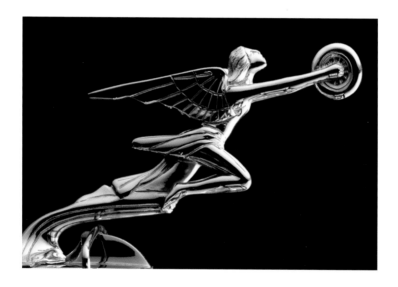

136 • A winged virgin holding a wheel is the emblem of this 1930 Packard 745 Convertible coupe.

137 • The nose of the 1930 Packard 850 roadster is instantly recognizable by the winged virgin ready to take flight.

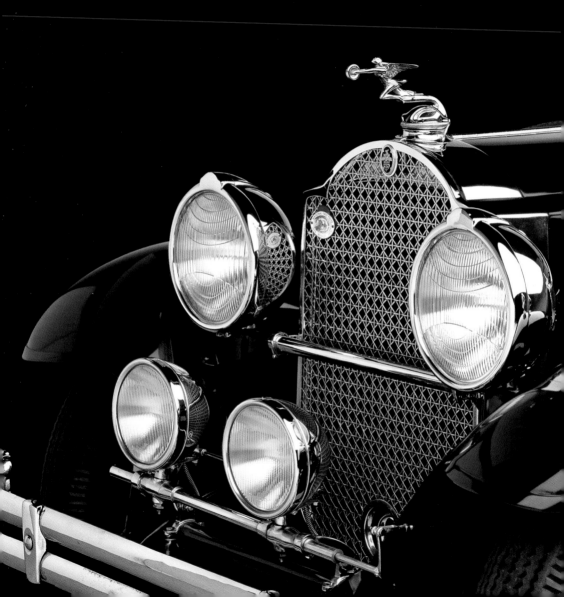

138 • The radiator cap of this 1931 Packard is adorned with a chrome putto mascot.

139 • Great freedom of expression was displayed on radiator caps, as testified by this "Spirit of the Wind."

140 • Like Packard, the mascot of the Milan manufacturer Isotta Fraschini was also a winged virgin holding a wheel.

141 • The mascot of this 1931 Buick Victoria Custom Convertible is a female figure ready to glide on the wind.

Mascots sometimes represented whimsical characters, such as that adorning the 1931
Bugatti Type 41, left, or this 1930 Isotta Fraschini Dual Cove Phaeton, right.

144 • This Packard Victoria's emblem is decidedly modern in style.

145 • The mascot of this 1933 Buick Packard Convertible CP is characterized by its spread wings.

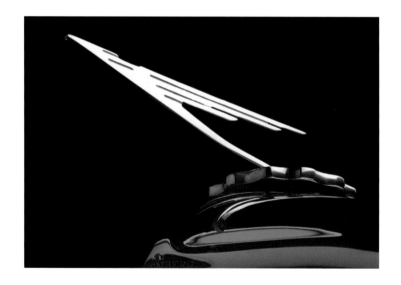

146 ● The stylized mascot of this 1931 Duesenberg Model SJ "French Speedster" is inspired by flight and gracefulness .

147 ● Auburn too yielded to the charm of winged virgins for its cars, such as this 1936 model.

148 • There was also room for warriors on radiator caps, as demonstrated by
this 1937 Pierce Arrow.

149 • The radiator of this 1931 Stutz Bearcat is adorned with an authentic chrome work of art.

150 • The rampant horse has always been the emblem of Porsche and is derived from the coat of arms of the city of Stuttgart.

151 • The "double kidney" radiator grille and the stylized propeller emblem are the typical motifs of BMW, shown here on a 328 (1936-1940).

152 • Never was a winged mascot more appropriate than on this 1936 Chrysler Airstream Convertible.

153 • The Auburn Cabriolet (1932-1935) has an imposing and rather squat hood ornament.

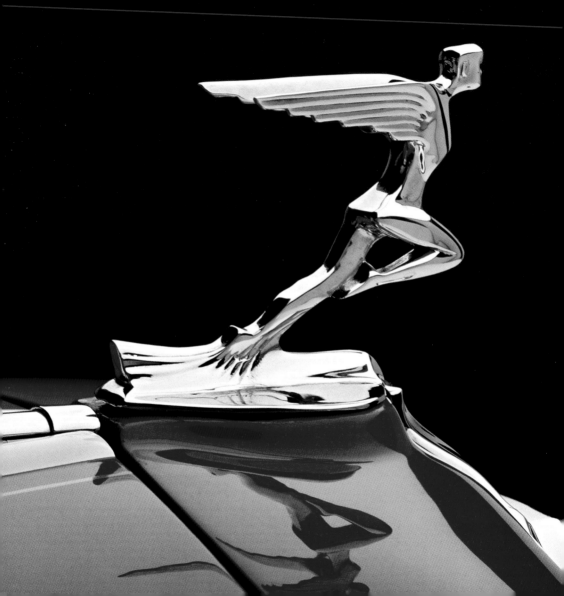

154 • The emblem of this 1940s Bentley Continental S-Type takes the form of a winged "B" on the radiator.

155 • A side view of the winged "B" adorning the radiator of the 1947 Bentley Shooting Brake.

156 • The refined Cadillac emblem adorning this 1953 El Dorado Convertible is worthy of the fame of its manufacturer.

157 • Mascots must be aerodynamic as well as elegant, like that of the Ford Lincoln Continental shown here.

The Mercedes star on a 1937 540k Special Roadster, left, and , like the sight of a fighter plane on a Mercedes Benz 540k Special Roadster, right.

160 • The mascot of this sporty 1946 Chevrolet V-8 reflects the red bodywork.

161 • The winged mascot of this 1931 Cadillac V16 Dual Cowl is as elegant as
the vehicle itself.

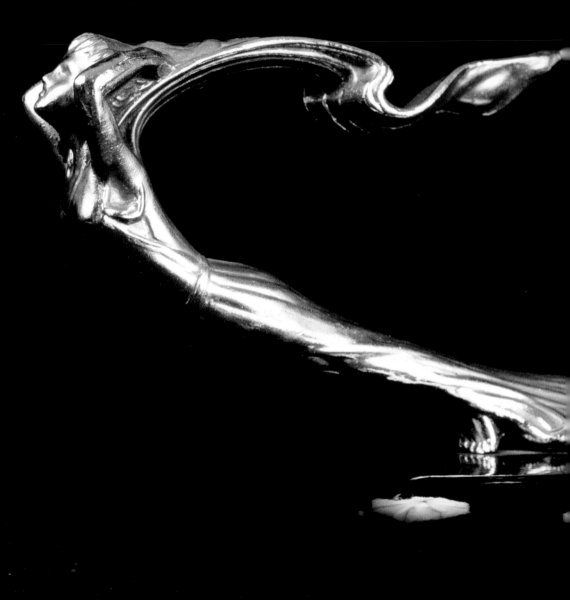

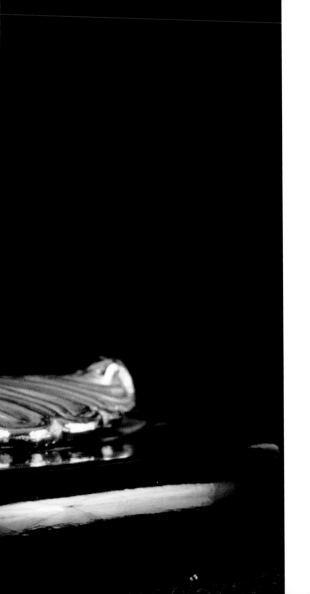

162-163 ● This goddess with hair streaming in the wind appears ready to take flight to emulate the theme of freedom.

163 ● Chrome statuettes such as this one, which dates back to the 1920s, also cut a fine figure in elegance contests.

164 • The "Spirit of Ecstasy" of the new Rolls-Royce 100 EX Cabriolet disappears
inside the radiator in the case of attempted theft.

165 • A close-up of the Rolls-Royce logo and mascot, shown here on
the convertible 100 EX.

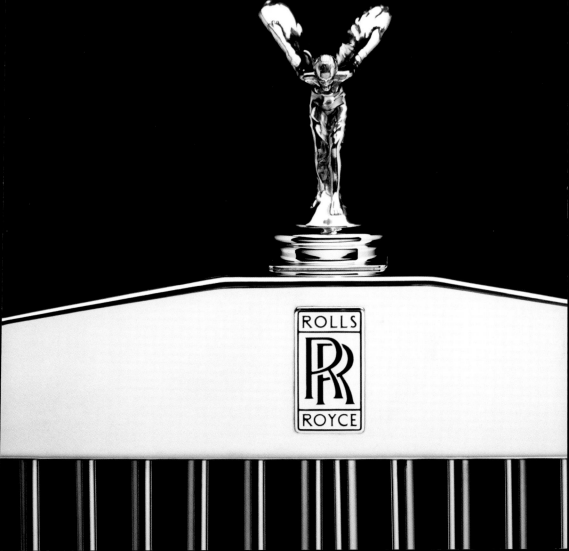

Jaguars, such as this 1959 MKII, left, and the 1948 Drophead, right, have always been distinguished by their radiator grilles, as well as the leaping jaguar emblem.

168 • The jaguar has always been the symbol of the British company of the same name and is featured in both the badge and the emblem of the MK.

168-169 • The jaguar was chosen by Sir Lyons, the company's founder, from a list of animals proposed by the Nelson agency.

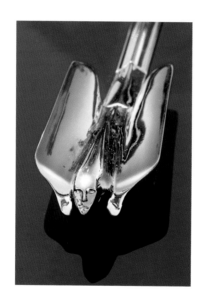

Detail of the hood emblem of a 1947 Cadillac. These devices were intended as lucky mascots.

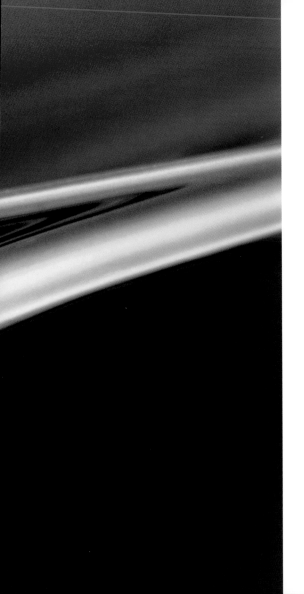

172-173 and 173 • Variations on the theme
of the wheel, such as the mascot of this
1949 Ford, left, or the 1950 Mercury, right.

174-175 • The mascot on this
late-1950s Pontiac is a tribute to
the Native Americans.

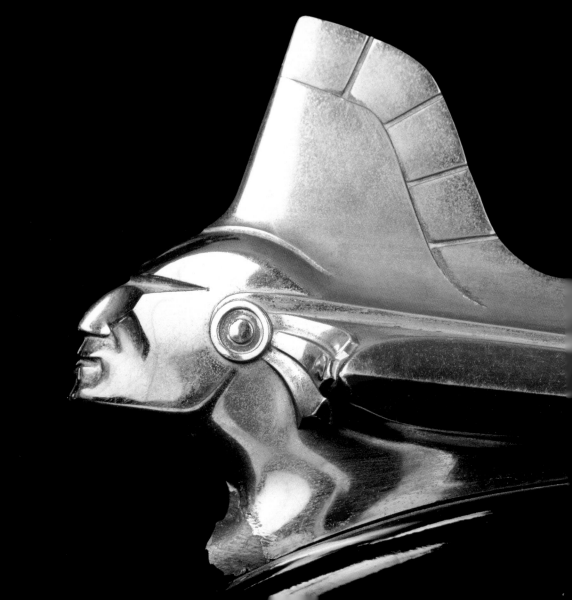

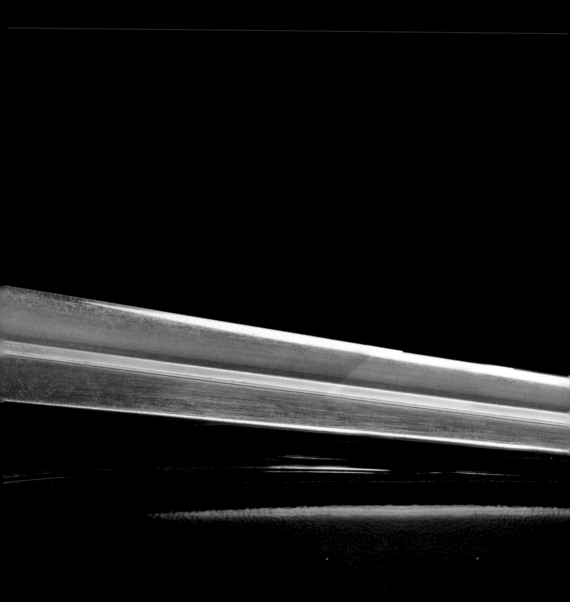

176 • The elegant hood emblem of this sporty 1937 Ford is inspired by marine themes.

177 • The chrome symbol of this 1938 Buick Road Master represents a jet engine.

178 • The eight-cylinder engine of this 1940 Ford V-8 is proclaimed on the front of the car.

179 • The Chevrolet cross appears on this 1938 Car Rally, produced in Southern California.

180 • A stylized eagle emblem identifies this 1956 Ford Thunderbird.

181 • The Chevrolet Camaro plaque adorns bodywork painted with typical Indy racing colors: blue with white stripes.

182 • The logo of the 1950 Oldsmobile Club Coupe features a globe bearing the two
Americas surrounded by Saturn-like rings.

183 • The tail of this Buick Centurion (1947-1952) is characterized by a conical tip.

184 • Racing is part of the genetic makeup of the 1963 Chevrolet Corvette, as shown by its shield.

185 • Another Corvette and its emblem: the Chevrolet cross on a red ground and the checkered flag.

186 • Emblems may even be featured on wing mirrors, as demonstrated by this 1978 Cadillac Eldorado.

187 • This emblem distinguishes the 1963 Cadillac Eldorado and the 1970s Fleetwoods.

188 • The most famous horse is that of Ferrari, shown here on the gas cap of the 2004 F360.

189 • The 2004 Ferrari F360 bears a yellow shield containing the prancing horse and the manufacturer's initials, topped by the colors of the Italian flag.

190 • The trident has always been Maserati's emblem, on both its road and its racing cars.

191 • The Maserati emblem also appears on the wheel hub of this GT racing car: the 2005 MC12.

NOBLE AND LUXURIOUS

- The unmistakable nose of a 1962 Rolls-Royce Silver Cloud.

INTRODUCTION Noble and Luxurious

ROLLS-ROYCE IS PRACTICALLY SYNONYMOUS WITH LUXURY CARS, NOW AS IN THE PAST. HOWEVER, THE DEFINING CHARACTERISTIC OF THESE CARS IS NOT MERELY THAT THEY REPRESENT THE VERY BEST IN TERMS OF LEATHER, WOOD, AND MECHANICAL AND ELECTRONIC TECHNOLOGIES, FOR IF THIS WERE THE CASE ANYONE WITH ADEQUATE MEANS WOULD BE ABLE TO PRODUCE THEM... IT IS INSTEAD NECESSARY TO KNOW HOW TO IDENTIFY, CHOOSE, AND COMBINE THE BEST. THE CURRENT ROLLS-ROYCE PHANTOM, THE ONLY LUXURY CAR THAT STILL RETAINS THE LINES OF THE VINTAGE MODELS, IS THE EXAMPLE IN STEEL AND HORSEPOWER OF WHAT KNOWING HOW TO CHOOSE REALLY MEANS: THE HIDES USED FOR THE

INTRODUCTION Noble and Luxurious

SEATS COME FROM FARMS THAT ARE PERSONALLY SE-LECTED AND MONITORED BY THE MANUFACTURER. THE ANIMALS ARE FED A HEALTHY DIET AND MAS-SAGED TO ENSURE THAT THEIR HIDES REMAIN SOFT AFTER TANNING. THE LAMBSKIN RUGS ON THE FLOOR OF THE PASSENGER COMPARTMENT ARE LUXURIOUS-LY DEEP AND INCOMPARABLY SOFT. THE PHANTOM AL-SO REPRESENTS THE BEST IN MECHANICAL AND TECH-NOLOGICAL TERMS, DRAWING ON ITS FAMILY TIES, I.E. EXPLOITING THE KNOW-HOW DEVELOPED AND TESTED ON OTHER CARS MANUFACTURED BY THE SAME GROUP. THE SAME PRACTICE IS, OF COURSE, FOL-LOWED BY OTHER LUXURY CAR MANUFACTURERS, WHICH ENABLES THEM TO CREATE "RICH MEN'S TOYS"

Noble and Luxurious

Introduction

THAT APPROACH TECHNICAL PERFECTION: ABSOLUTE-LY SILENT CARS, WHERE THE MAIN PASSENGER RIDES ON A SEAT THAT BECOMES A CHAISE LONGUE WITH BUILT-IN MASSAGE FUNCTION.

MERCEDES, MAYBACH (RECENTLY REVIVED BY DAIM-LER-CHRYSLER), JAGUAR, BENTLEY, AUDI, LANCIA, AND CADILLAC ARE THE QUINTESSENTIAL LUXURY CARS. THE LIST CAN BE EXTENDED WITH NAMES OF THE PAST LIKE ISOTTA FRASCHINI OR DUESENBERG, AND NEW ENTRIES FROM JAPAN, SUCH AS LEXUS, INFINITI, AND ACURA – THE LUXURY DIVISIONS OF TOYOTA, NISSAN, AND HONDA RESPECTIVELY.

197 ● The tips of the fins of the 1956 Lincoln Mark II are formed by the taillights.

198-199 ● The color of this 1948 Bentley is decidedly bizarre.

200-201 ● This elegant Jaguar is the 1948 Drophead 3.5.

202 and 203 • The Alfa Romeo 6C2500SS (1947-1951) features a monocoque body with built-in fenders and lights.

204-205 • The single passenger compartment and full roof help to give this 1950 Rolls-Royce Silver Wraith a truly solid, yet well-balanced appearance, like a sculpture.

206-207 • One of Lancia's jewels: the Aurelia B20GT Coupe.

208-209 ● The nose of this distinguished 1953 Cadillac Ghia Coupe gives it a touch of aggressiveness.

210-211 ● This Bentley Continental S-Type coupe (1956-1959) is characterized by sleek, elegant lines.

212-213 ● The 1956 Mark II is squared, low-slung, and shamelessly American in its dimensions.

214-215 • An open sports car in the most classic British tradition – a Jaguar XK150 (1957-1961).

216-217 • The classic Greek temple–style radiator adorns the 1959 Rolls-Royce Silver Cloud II.

218-219 • The divine 1959 Citroën DS is both alluring and extraordinary contemporary.

220-221 • The body of this Lancia Flaminia 2500 (1959-1961) was designed by Zagato.

222-223 • The E-type – in this case a late-1950s MK 2 – is the most famous and sought-after Jaguar by collectors.

224-225 • The 1967 Eldorado – shown here in the coupe version – is an icon of both the United States and Cadillac.

226-227 • The 1971 Mercedes Benz 280 SE Coupe features a large chrome radiator grille and six headlights.

The 1971 Mercedes 280SE Coupe is very well proportioned.

230-231 • The 1971 Rolls-Royce Corniche Convertible emerged unscathed from the years of the oil crisis.

232-233 • The profile of the Cadillac Seville (1980-1985) is characterized by the spare tire compartment.

234-235 • The 2004 Bentley Continental GT Silver has an extremely alluring design.

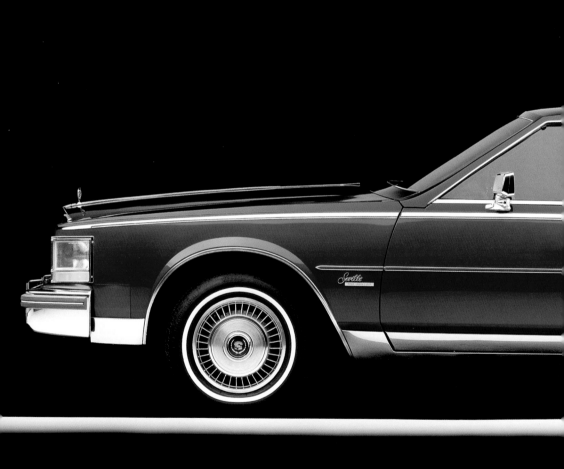

236-237 • Bentley's sumptuous invention for the third millennium: the 2000 Azure Mulliner.

238-239 • The 2005 Maserati Quattroporte Silver is the sporty flagship worthy of the House of the Trident.

FIFTIES
FOLLIES

● This imposing 1953 Buick Skylark is a triumph of chrome work and bumper bullets.

INTRODUCTION Fifties Follies

FOLLOWING THE WAR, PEOPLE WISHED TO FORGET THE MISERY AND PAIN OF THE CONFLICT AS QUICKLY AS POSSIBLE. THIS WAS TRUE IN BOTH EUROPE AND AMERICA. MAN'S INBUILT INSTINCT OF SURVIVAL TRIGGERED A REBIRTH, WHICH EXPRESSED THE JOY THAT FOLLOWS PAIN AND THE WISH TO RETURN TO NORMAL LIFE. FROM A MOTORING POINT OF VIEW, THIS WIDESPREAD DESIRE FOR PROSPERITY CULMINATED IN THE DOLCE VITA OF THE 1950S AND '60S AND IN *AMERICAN GRAFFITI*. FUN, JOY, LIGHTHEARTEDNESS, AND A YEARNING FOR LAUGHTER ARE ALL EXPRESSED IN THE CARS THAT BECAME THE ICONS OF THE PERIOD AND OF AN INDISPUTEDLY AMERICAN MODEL, AND WHICH STILL MAKE US SMILE TODAY. THEIR NAMES WERE CADILLAC ELDORA-

INTRODUCTION Fifties Follies

DO, OLDSMOBILE 98, BUICK SKYLARK, PACKARD, FORD THUNDERBIRD, CHRYSLER NEWYORKER AND IMPERIAL, AND FORD SKYLINER. ALMOST ALL OF THEM WERE CONVERTIBLES AND HAD THE TASK OF EMBODYING THE NEW MOTORING TREND, CONSTITUTED BY OVERSIZED MODELS, CHROME WORK, GLEAMING PAINT, AND A PLETHORA OF WHAT WERE OFTEN USELESS AIR VENTS. HOWEVER, THE REAL SYMBOLS OF THE PERIOD WERE FINS: SIMILAR TO THOSE OF AIRPLANES AND CONCENTRATED AT THE TAIL OF THE CAR. AT LAST, TAILS TOO WERE IMPOSING, DIGNIFIED BY THESE PROMINENT, UNCONVENTIONAL, AND EYE-CATCHING FEATURES, ALONG WITH THE LIGHTS THAT CLUNG TO THEIR TIPS. FINS CHARACTERIZED THE AMERICAN CARS PRODUCED DURING THE TWO DECADES

Fifties Follies

Introduction

FOLLOWING THE SECOND WORLD WAR. THEIR MIGRA-
TION FROM AIRPLANES – WHERE THEIR EXISTENCE WAS
JUSTIFIED ON AERODYNAMIC GROUNDS – TO CARS FOR
MERELY COSMETIC REASONS CAN BE ATTRIBUTED TO A
BRILLIANT DESIGNER CALLED HARLEY EARL. HOWEVER,
THE NEW APPEARANCE OF CARS WAS ALSO INFLUENCED
BY DESIGN IN OTHER FIELDS. A PRIME EXAMPLE OF THIS IS
THE OLDSMOBILE 98, WHOSE TAIL IS SO PROMINENT AS
TO RECALL THE STERN OF A YACHT. IN THIS CASE THE
"NAUTICAL" EFFECT IS REINFORCED BY ANOTHER CON-
TRIVANCE, FOR THE SPARE WHEEL IS FASTENED TO THE
SURFACE LIKE THE LIFE BELT OF A MOTORBOAT, BY
MEANS OF A CHROMED AND COLORED COVER.

- Large fins and headlights resembling reptilian eyes make the 1958
Chevrolet Impala absolutely unique.

246-247 • Perhaps the most extreme fins in history are those of the 1959 Cadillac Fleetwood 60 Special.

248-249 and 250-251 • The top of this Cadillac Eldorado partially covers the passengers, like the Sedancas produced at the turn of the twentieth century.

252-253 • The austere 1949 Cadillac Sedanette Fastback features a distinctive "brow" above the windshield.

254 and 255 • The Cadillac Custom Cadstar has fins, although they are not very accentuated, and chrome bumperettes that sprout from the radiator grille to develop into bumpers.

256-257 • The 1954 Cadillac Custom Cadstar is very low-slung.

258-259 • The 1954 Cadillac Eldorado: the icon of the era made famous by *American Graffiti*.

260-261 • The color of this 1953 Buick Skylark is sober and elegant.

262-263 • This 1957 Mercury Turnpike Cruiser features an unusual four-door body.

264-265 • Two-tone bodywork was another distinctive feature of the period, as shown by the 1956 Buick Century.

266-267 • The Bel Air,
Chevrolet's answer to
the Cadillac Eldorado,
featured large tail fins.

268-269 •
The Tucker Torpedo
is characterized by
rounded forms and
chromework.

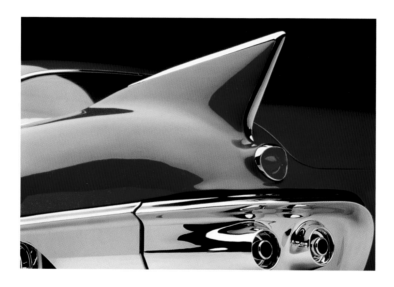

270 • Variations on the theme of fins: here they appear in a tamer guise
on the 1957 Cadillac Eldorado.

271 • The nose of the 1957 Cadillac Eldorado features extensive chromework
and extra headlights.

272-273 ● The chrome radiator grille with bumper bullets of the 1957 Cadillac Sedan de Ville resembles the gaping mouth of a whale.

273 ● The taillights of the 1957 Cadillac Sedan de Ville are set in the lower part of the fin.

274-275 ● The Cadillac 62 has very clean lines – except, of course, for the tail.

276-277 ● This low-slung, aggressive-looking 1950 Buick Sedanette features a rare sedan body.

278-279
Chrome noses, such as
this belonging to the
Cadillac Eldorado Series
62, are characteristic of
1950s American cars.

280-281 • A close-up
of the tail fin, which also
houses the space-age
lights of the 1959
Cadillac Eldorado.

282-283 •
The huge oval radiator
grille of the Ford Edsel
is reminiscent of a jet
engine.

284-285 • The 1953
Cadillac Eldorado did
not yet feature fins,
although the
chromework was
already there.

● The paintwork of the 1957 Chrysler Imperial Crown Coupe is completely metallic, apart from the roof.

The profile of the 1956 Buick Centurion reveals a rounded nose and bizarre tail.

290 • The futuristic 1956 Buick Centurion has a space-age tail.

291 • The show-stopping exterior of the Buick Centurion was matched on the inside by a screen for the rear video camera.

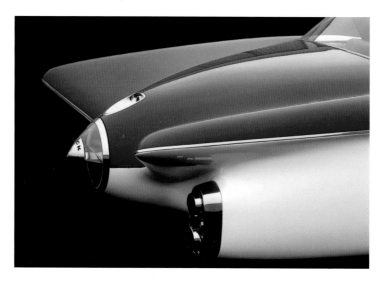

292-293 • The only things missing from this 1956 candy pink Packard are the pinups.

294-295 • This 1954 Cadillac Eldorado Convertible is well over 17 feet long.

FAST AND SPORTY

Ferdinand Porsche's masterpiece, the 911, is still produced today in its original form.

INTRODUCTION Fast and Sporty

Some are born for the road, but would feel equally at home on the track. Others are designed for racing and are subsequently converted for "civilian" use. We are talking about sports cars: the category of cars that, along with the great sedans, or flagships, represents the best of the technology available to a car manufacturer and the tangible form of years of research and enormous investment by the brand. As they are high-performance vehicles, their results are assessed in terms of their feats. At least this was the case at first, and up until recently. However, today things have changed and sports cars are the highest expression of the

INTRODUCTION Fast and Sporty

CULTURE AND POWER EXPRESSED BY A BRAND, AND IN THIS NEW MILLENNIUM PERFORMANCE IS INCREASINGLY EXPECTED TO GO HAND IN HAND WITH LUXURY AND COMFORT. INDEED, OVER THE PAST TWENTY YEARS SPORTS CARS HAVE GAINED A NEW SPLENDOR IN A FORMIDABLE REVIVAL OF THE 1950S AND '60S, WHEN THE MODELS WERE CERTAINLY SPORTY BUT UNCOMFORTABLE AND BASIC. THIS IS THE STORY OF THE CAR: ONCE THE RELIABILITY AND MECHANICAL RESISTANCE OF THE VEHICLES HAVE BEEN TESTED, THEN THEY MUST START TO OFFER PERFORMANCE AND SPEED – COMFORT ONLY COMES LATER.

THE LEGENDARY SPORTS CARS ARE TIMELESS; THEY ARE MAINLY COUPES WITH AERODYNAMIC LINES (SOMETIMES

Fast and Sporty

Introduction

FUTURISTIC LIKE THE ALFA ROMEO DISCO VOLANTE), VERY LOW, WITH JUST TWO SEATS OR AT MOST 2+2 AND A RECLINING DRIVING POSITION TO FEEL THE ROAD AT CLOSE QUARTERS. FIRST PLACE IN THE LINEUP IS OCCUPIED BY FERRARI AND PORSCHE, FOLLOWED BY LAMBORGHINI AND BUGATTI (REVIVED BY VOLKSWAGEN), THEN LOTUS, ASTON MARTIN, JAGUAR, AND MODELS LIKE THE CHEVROLET CORVETTE, FORD MUSTANG, AND PONTIAC FIREBIRD. ALL OF THEM DISPLAY THEIR MUSCLES AS THEY RACE ALONG THE ROAD AT OVER 185 MPH. THE LATEST, AFTER VARIOUS ORDEALS, IS A REBORN LEGEND: THE BUGATTI VEYRON, 16 CYLINDERS, 1,000 HP, AND 250 MPH TO EAT UP THE MILES AND ALLOW US TO DREAM ONCE AGAIN.

301 • From 1985 to 1994 the F40 was Ferrari's fastest and most extreme road car.

302-303 • Elegance and sobriety are characteristics of the 1953 MG TF 1250 roadster.

304 • The Cisitalia Gran Sport – shown here in the closed version – had racing in its blood.

305 • A rear view of the open version of the Cisitalia Gran Sport, which retains the two seats, but does away with the top.

306-307 • The Ferrari 166, produced in late 1948, adopted the philosophy of the British roadsters.

308-309 • The classic Jaguar XK120 (1948-1954), shown here in cabriolet version.

310 • The elegant Italian answer to the 1950s British roadsters: the Lancia Aurelia B20.

311 • The Lancia Aurelia B20, which was also highly acclaimed on the other side of the Atlantic, boasted a particularly imposing nose.

312 • The MG TF (1953-1955)
had a rather square tail to
accommodate the spare tire.

312-313 • Another MG roadster,
with a very classic design:
the TC, produced between
1953 and 1955.

The Triumph TR3A (1958-1961) is another icon of British roadsters and featured a very innovative design for its day.

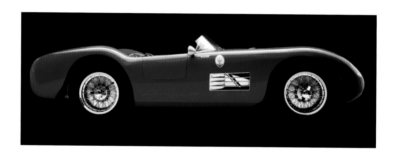

316 • As its name suggests, the no-frills Maserati Sportiva was designed to offer high performance.

317 • A classic 1950s Maserati: the 1954 A6G.

The Alfa Romeo
Giulietta Spider was an
icon of the dolce vita of
1950s Italy, along with
the Lancia Aurelia B20
and B24.

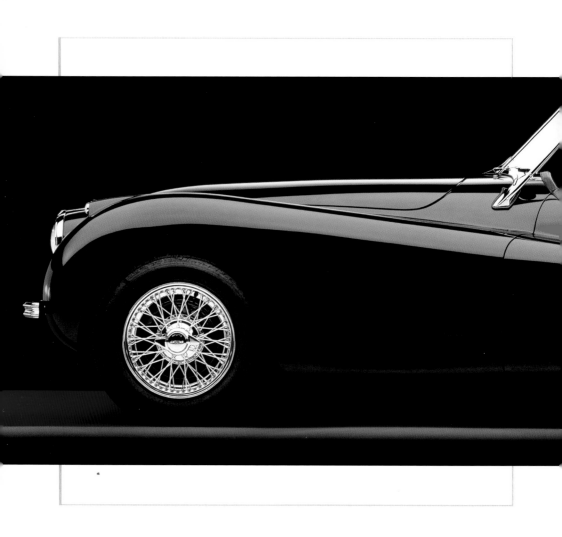

This 1954 Jaguar XK120 M Roadster is characterized by its elegant dark bodywork and sinuous design.

322-323 • Timeless elegance: the Mercedes 300SL Gullwing is a benchmark for sports cars.

324-325 • The 1958 Chevrolet Corvette, shown here in an elegant yellow livery, was the American answer to Porsche and Ferrari.

326-327 • A close-up of the nose of the quintessential American sports car: the Chevrolet Corvette (1959).

328-329 • The Ford Thunderbird has tail fins and a spare tire compartment on the trunk.

330-331 • The 1957 Porsche GS/GT Carrera Speedster Convertible has a Teutonic charm.

332-333 and 333 • An example
of a British roadster, shown here
with two-tone bodywork: the
Austin Healey 100M (1955-1956).

334-335 • This splendid black
MGA Roadster features spoked
wheels with whitewall tires.

336-337 • This 1960s Jaguar
XK-E coupe has a timeless charm.

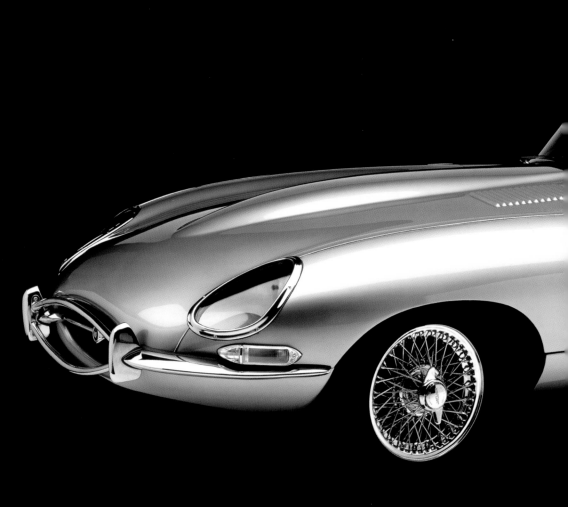

338 • The name of the Ferrari 250GT California Spider hinted at the United States, the car's main market.

339 • The nose of the Ferrari 250 (1959-1962) , shown here in the coupe version. This car has always been a sought-after collector's piece.

340-341 • The Mustang (1964) is Ford's sports car par excellence and takes its name from the American wild horse.

342-343 • A special version of the Chevrolet Corvette, the Mako Shark, which was clearly inspired by its namesake.

344-345 • The 1967 AC Cobra 427CSX: a sports car with a large radiator grille for more efficient engine cooling.

346-347 • The Lamborghini Miura (1966-1969). The Volkswagen Group, which owns the brand, is currently designing its successor.

348-349 • The Alfa Romeo Duetto (1966-1967) – also known as the Osso di Seppia ("Cuttlefish Bone") – is the quintessential Italian sports car.

350-351 and 351 • The Ferrari Dino 206GT (1964-1974) was dedicated to the memory of Enzo Ferrari's son. It shared its engine with the Fiat Dino.

352-353 • A 1988 Porsche 911 Turbo, shown here in the cabriolet version.

354-355 • The Ferrari Testarossa was the point of reference for the sports cars of the 1970s and '80s and is an essential piece for any collector.

● This exuberant Lamborghini Countach LP5000S QV (1985-1990) features gullwing doors.

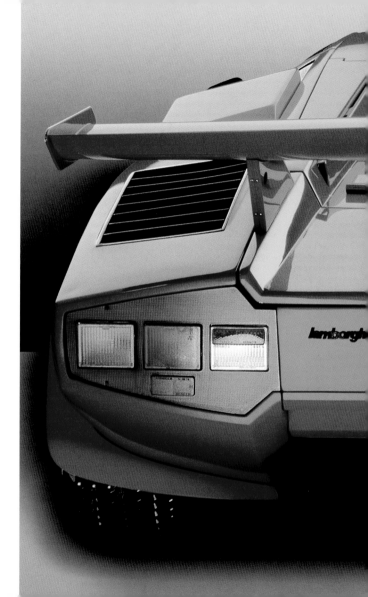

358-359 • The extremely powerful 1985 Lamborghini Countach 5000S is characterized by a large rear spoiler.

360-361 • The Bugatti EB110 made its debut in 1993. The brand purchased by Romano Artioli was subsequently bought out by the Volkswagen Group.

362-363 • This Bugatti EB110GT (1992-1995) boasts blue livery, like the racing color of France.

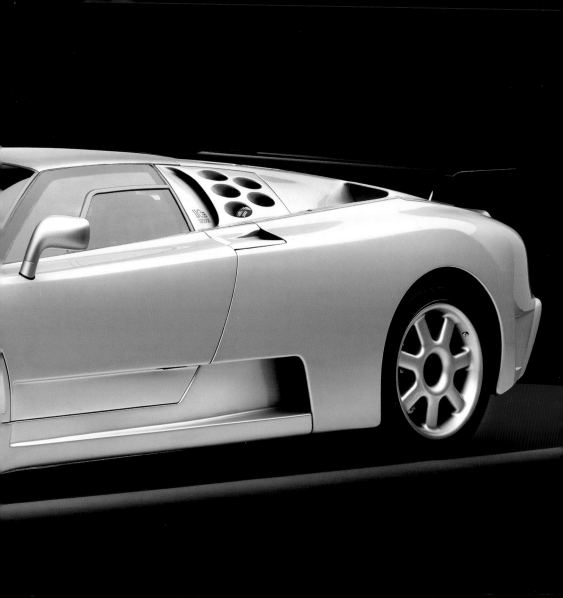

364-365 • The Ferrari F355 was produced between 1994 and 1999, before being replaced by the F360.

365 • A rear three-quarter view of the Ferrari F355 Spider in the classic red color.

366-367 • The silver bodywork heightens the impression of power in this 1995 Lamborghini Diablo VT with all-wheel drive.

368-369 • The 1990s Dodge Viper is a sports car without compromises and is not equipped with any electronic driving systems.

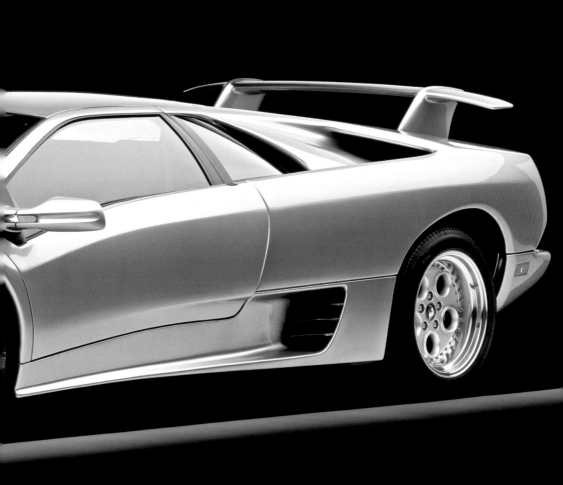

370-371 • A Formula One racing car converted for road use: the 1995 McLaren F1.

371 • The gullwing doors are one of the quirks of the 1995 McLaren F1.

372-373 • The 1997 F50 successfully took up the baton from the F40, immortalizing the Ferrari legend.

374-375 • Although the 1997 BMW Z3 was developed as a prototype, the interest that it aroused at motor shows resulted in it becoming a successful mass-produced model.

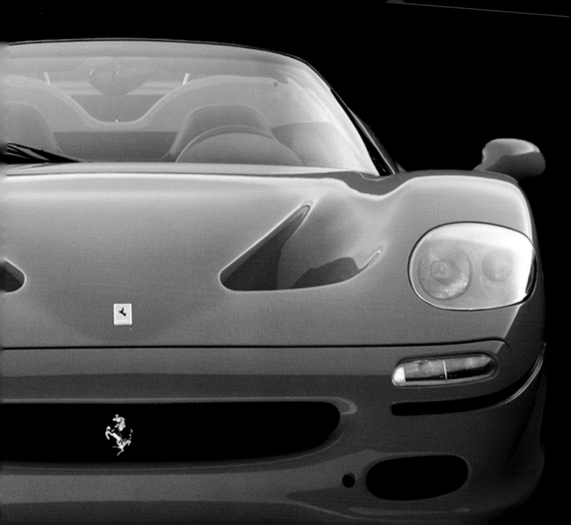

376-377 • The Porsche Boxster, shown here in the sporty S version, made its debut in 1999 and represents an alternative to the timeless 911.

377 • The name of this Porsche – Boxtster – was obtained by merging the words boxer (engine) and roadster (body).

378-379 • The various generations of Chevrolet Corvette have been a constant presence on the motoring scene.

380-381 • The top-of-the-range BMW roadster: the 2000 Z8, also driven by James Bond.

382-383 • The 2002 Ferrari Enzo has inherited much from Formula One racing.

384-385 • The 2001 Saleen S7 is an American sports car that is also seeking success in Europe.

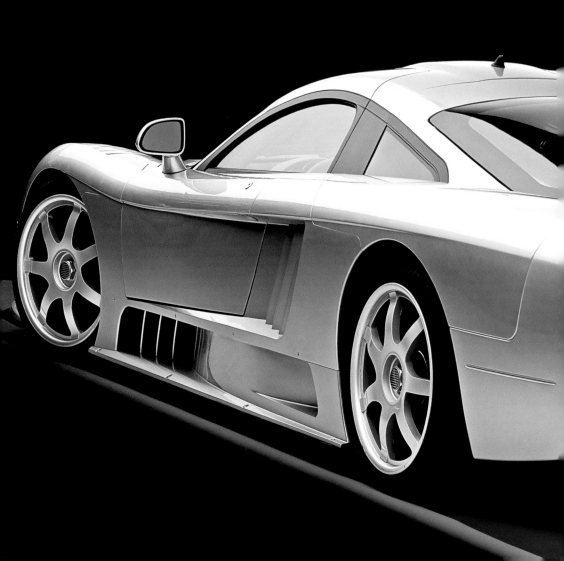

386 and 386-387 • The 2002 Ferrari Modena is the coupe version of the F360 and represented the entry-level Ferrari until the arrival of the F340.

388-389 • Another quintessential sports car in yellow livery: the 2002 Chevrolet Corvette Z06 Avelate.

390-391 • This 2003 Maserati Spider features an V8 engine.

The latest-generation Chevrolet Corvette, which made its debut in 2005, features exposed headlights.

394-395 and 395 • The 2004 Porsche Carrera GT features a roadster body with removable top and a 10-cylinder engine.

396-397 • Mercedes' muscle car is the 2005 SLR, which features gullwing doors like the 300SI.

398-399 • The 2005 Ford GT marks the great return of an historic American sports car.

400-401 • A special version of a special car: the 2005 Dodge Hennessey Viper.

402-403 • The 2005 MC12 is the star of the lineup in Maserati's great return to the racetrack.

404-405 • The 2005 Aston Martin DB9 coupe is a timeless British sports car.

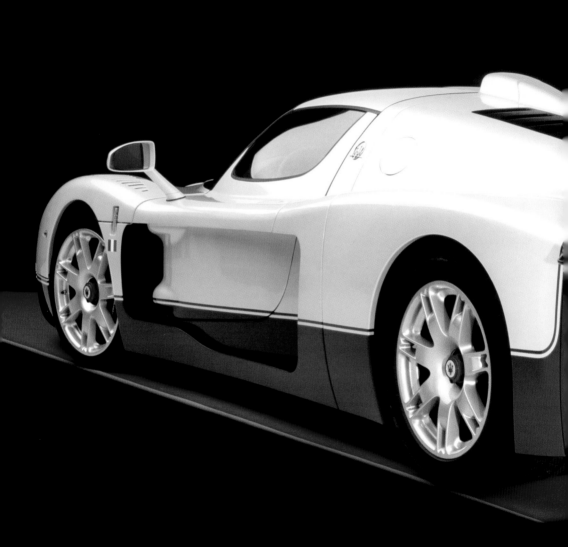

GREAT LITTLE CARS

- The 1946 Volkswagen Type 1 Beetle: Ferdinand Porsche was the "father" of this four-wheeled legend.

INTRODUCTION Great Little Cars

THEY BOAST NO REFINED TECHNICAL FEATURES AND HAVE LITTLE TO OFFER IN THE WAY OF PERFORMANCE. SIMILARLY, THEIR DESIGN LEAVES MUCH TO BE DESIRED AND THE FINISHINGS OF THEIR INTERIORS AND QUALITY OF THEIR MATERIALS ARE OFTEN NOTHING TO WRITE HOME ABOUT. RUNABOUTS WERE INVENTED BY CAR MANUFACTURERS TO TARGET THE GENERAL PUBLIC WITH THE AIM OF ACHIEVING MAXIMUM RESULTS (PRACTICALITY AND WIDE DIFFUSION) AT MINIMUM EXPENSE (LOW PRODUCTION COSTS), ALTHOUGH THE RESULTS WERE ACTUALLY SOMETIMES AUTHENTIC MASTERPIECES. THE NAME "RUNABOUTS" DOES NOT DO JUSTICE TO THE TRUE ESSENCE OF THESE CARS AND THEIR WIDESPREAD DIFFUSION ALONE DOES NOT JUSTIFY THEIR SUCCESS. WHAT WAS NEEDED WERE THE BRILLIANT IDEAS

INTRODUCTION Great Little Cars

AND REVOLUTIONARY NOTIONS THAT ENABLED MEN LIKE ALEC ISSIGONIS OR DANTE GIOCOSA TO CREATE SOMETHING EXTRAORDINARY THAT IS STILL AT THE CUTTING EDGE TODAY – FIFTY YEARS DOWN THE ROAD. ISSIGONIS WAS THE MAN WHO DESIGNED THE MINI, WHOSE SPIRIT AND FORM HAVE SURVIVED UNALTERED TO THE PRESENT DAY. HOWEVER, AT THE TIME OF ITS DEBUT THE CAR AROUSED LITTLE ENTHUSIASM, ESPECIALLY WITH REGARD TO ITS APPEARANCE. AT THE BEGINNING OF THE 1960S, JOHN COOPER TRAVELED TO THE MONZA GRAND PRIX ABOARD HIS MINI AND ALLOWED FIAT'S HEAD DESIGNER TO TRY IT OUT. FOLLOWING A TEST DRIVE, THE ITALIAN REALIZED THAT HE WAS DEALING WITH A REVOLUTIONARY CAR, BUT ADDED, "FORTUNATELY FOR FIAT, IT'S UGLY." THE FIAT 500, WITH ITS UGLY DUCKLING

Great Little Cars
introduction

APPEARANCE, ALSO RECEIVED LITTLE ACCLAIM. HOWEVER, IT SEATED FOUR PEOPLE AND HAD REAR-WHEEL DRIVE AND SUFFICIENT HORSEPOWER. OTHER GREAT LITTLE MOTORING MASTERPIECES INCLUDE THE CITROËN 2CV, THE RENAULT 4, AND THE VOLKSWAGEN BEETLE, DESIGNED BY FERDINAND PORSCHE, WHO DEVISED A MECHANICAL LAYOUT THAT SUBSEQUENTLY BECAME PART OF THE GENETIC MAKEUP OF MODELS SUCH AS THE 356 AND 911. THE NUMBER OF LITTLE GEMS HAS INCREASED OVER THE YEARS, WITH ROADSTERS (THE MGA AND THE MAZDA MX-5 "MIATA"), HATCHBACKS (VOLKSWAGEN GOLF), AND MICROCARS, SUCH AS THE SMART. WE EAGERLY AWAIT THE NEW GENERATIONS…

The 1959 Austin Seven Mini: the basic shapes and volumes remain unchanged in the current model.

412-413 • The Fiat Topolino is the symbol of the runabouts of the period.

413 • A rear three-quarter view of the Fiat Topolino, shown here with fabric top and two-tone bodywork.

414-415 • France too had its own great little car, which boasted an exceptionally futuristic design: the Citroën2CV.

415 • The 2CV has an appealing, jaunty appearance. The hole beneath the logo on the radiator grille could be used to crank start the car.

416-417 • The Fiat 500 was the car that motorized postwar Italy and is now a highly sought-after collector's piece.

418-419 • The 1960s Renault 4 was an alternative interpretation of the concept embodied by the Citroën2CV.

The indestructible Trabant, with plastic bodywork, is an Eastern European icon.

422 • This Volkswagen Beetle was produced in 1970 and was also available in a cabriolet version.

422-423 • Chrome work was also featured on the Beetle, as in the 1970 version shown here, and extended to the bumpers.

The Volkswagen Golf GTi, shown here in a 1986 version, has been a point of reference for low-cost GT cars since the mid-1970s.

426-427 and 427 ● At just 8.2 feet long, the Smart City Cabrio – subsequently renamed the Smart ForTwo – is the smallest cabriolet on the road.

428-429 ● Relaunched by BMW, the Mini – shown here in the 2002 Cooper S version – has repeated the success of the first generation.

430-431 ● The New Beetle has not yet managed to repeat the success of the original version.

ROAD RACES

A Mitsubishi Pajero Evolution descending a dune during the 2005 Barcelona–Dakar Rally.

INTRODUCTION Road Races

Originally the new invention could only be used and tested on surfaced roads, which were often dusty, uneven, and closed to carriages or – as we would say today – "to private traffic." However, only a small proportion of public roads are now used for racing, which has been relegated to racetracks and circuits, while the main roads are still the settings for rallies, reenactments of historic races with the old glories of yesteryear, and a handful of uphill competitions. The sole exception is the city circuit of Monaco, which becomes a Formula One racetrack on occasion of the Monte Carlo Grand Prix. The advent of motoring at the end of the nineteenth century marked

INTRODUCTION Road Races

THE FORCEFUL IRRUPTION OF SPEED, MECHANICS, AND MODERNITY INTO MAN'S LIFE, SNATCHING HIM FROM THE SLOW RHYTHMS OF NATURE, FAMILIAR HORIZONS, AND WELL-KNOWN GOALS, AND DRIVING HIM TOWARDS THE NEW, THE UNKNOWN, AND THE UNPREDICTABLE. EARLY RACES WERE MORE LIKE DISPLAYS OF THE INDIVIDUAL MODEL THAN SPEED CONTESTS, AND MORE TRIALS OF MECHANICAL RESISTANCE OF THE NEW MEANS OF TRANSPORT THAN ATTEMPTS TO BREAK RECORDS. FURTHERMORE, CARS WERE MORE TOYS FOR THE WEALTHY THAN PROTOTYPES TO RACE. THEIR HORSEPOWER WAS INITIALLY EXPRESSED IN RACES FROM ONE CITY TO ANOTHER, COVERING EVER-INCREASING DISTANCES IN EVER-SHORTER TIMES. FRANCE WAS THE CRADLE OF THESE CONTESTS,

Road Races

AND THE VERY FIRST, HELD ON JULY 22, 1894, FEATURED TWO CARS RACING BETWEEN PARIS AND ROUEN. HOWEVER, THE FIRST TRUE ORGANIZED RACE WAS NOT STAGED UNTIL THE FOLLOWING YEAR: THE FIRST RALLY IN HISTORY WAS THE PARIS–BORDEAUX THAT TOOK PLACE ON JUNE 11, 1895. THE MOST FAMOUS ROAD RACES OF THE TWENTIETH CENTURY WERE THE TARGA FLORIO, MILLE MIGLIA, AND TOURIST TROPHY. THESE CONTESTS DREW CROWDS ALONG THEIR COURSES – CRAMMING THE MOST SPECTACULAR BENDS AND PERCHING ON ADVERTISING HOARDINGS – TO FORM A NARROW CHAIN LINKING PEOPLE HUNDREDS OF MILES APART, BUT UNITED BY RACING FEVER.

437 • Dirt tracks, mud, and even fords are all characteristics of the East African Rally.

438-439 • This buggy participating in the 2004 UAE Desert Challenge is almost hidden by the sand raised by its wheels.

Mexico

440 ● A Citroën Xsara in precarious equilibrium during a stage of the 2005 Rally Mexico.

440-441 ● A Ford Focus RS with its front wheels in the air following a jump during the 2005 Rally Mexico.

442 • A Japanese car in Latin America:
a Subaru Impreza engaged in the 2005
Rally Mexico.

442-443 • The queen of rallies, the
Subaru Impreza, during a rocky stage of
the 2005 Rally Mexico.

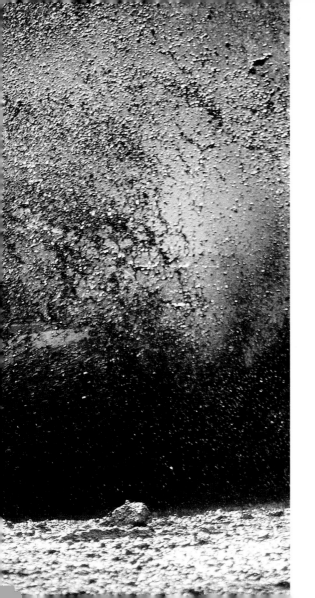

Australia

444-445 • A Subaru Impreza countersteering in the mud during one of the grueling legs of the Rally Australia.

445 • This airborne Ford Focus RS seems to be imitating the leap of a kangaroo during the Rally Australia.

446 • Many of the stages of the
2004 Rally Australia took place on
red dirt, like the terrain being
tackled by this Subaru Impreza.

446-447 • Skoda also participated
in the 2005 Rally Australia, as
demonstrated by this Fabia.

Sweden

• A Mitsubishi Lancer Evo 6 flying over the icy expanses in the 2005 Swedish Rally.

● A Subaru Impreza
countersteering a turn
in the 2004 Swedish
Rally.

452 • Almost the entire Swedish Rally takes place on ice and snow; a Mitsubishi Lancer Evo 7 during the 2001 event.

452-453 • A Peugeot 206 tackling a turn during the 2001 Swedish Rally.

Safari Rally

454-455 • Boundless horizons await this Ford Focus in the 2001 Safari Rally.

455 • A Subaru Impreza fording a river during the 2001 Safari Rally.

● Another leading name in rally history: the Mitsubishi Lancer Evo 7, shown here during the Safari Rally.

New Zealand
Rally

New Zealand, with its
breathtaking panoramas, is
another regular fixture of the
World Rally Championship: a
Subaru Impreza, left, racing
against a Citroën Xsara, right.

Great Britain

460 ● A Subaru Impreza tackling a muddy track beneath the pouring rain during the 2005 Wales Rally GB.

460-461 ● The Subaru Impreza rounding a turn in the 2005 Wales Rally GB.

Cyprus

462 • This Mitsubishi Lancer has an aversion to tarmac and is shown here tackling the dirt tracks of the 2005 Cyprus Rally.

463 • The forecarriage of a Citroën Xsara getting some rough treatment at the 2005 Cyprus Rally.

464-465 • A Peugeot 307 leaving a sandstorm in its tracks at the 2005 Cyprus Rally.

Turkey

466-467 • Not just barren landscapes, but also greenery with mountains in the distance, form the backdrop for this Subaru Impreza engaged in the 2005 Rally of Turkey.

467 • A Subaru Impreza WRC rounding a turn in the 2005 Rally of Turkey.

468 • A television crew risks a soaking as this Subaru Impreza speeds past in the 2005 Rally of Turkey.

469 • A Subaru Impreza leaves a shower of stones and gravel in its tracks during the 2005 Rally of Turkey.

Acropolis

470 ● Greece is another stage in the World Rally Championship: a Mitsubishi Lancer at the 2005 Acropolis Rally.

470-471 ● A challenging moment for car and crew: the Citroën Xsara at the Acropolis Rally 2005.

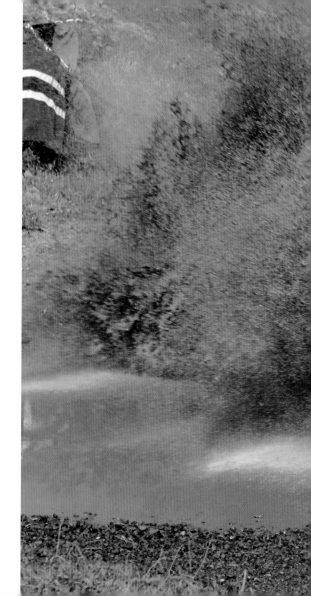

The tracks left by this Subaru Impreza at the 2005 Acropolis Rally reveal the tortuous course that it is tackling.

The Dakar

- A Volkswagen Tuareg fording a river during the grueling 2005 Barcelona–Dakar Rally.

476 ● A Mitsubishi Pajero Evolution scales a dune during the 2005 Barcelona–Dakar Rally.

476-477 ● If a vehicle stops on these dunes it will be unable to move again. Here, a Mitsubishi Pajero Evolution during the 2005 Barcelona–Dakar Rally.

478 • A Nissan Pickup climbing a dune at top speed during the 2005 Barcelona–Dakar Rally.

479 • A Volkswagen Tuareg modified for rallies during a stage of the 2005 Barcelona–Dakar Rally.

480-481 • A Nissan Pickup leaving a village during the 2005 Barcelona–Dakar Rally.

482-483 • A Range Rover in the yellow livery of a famous brand of cigarettes races across the sand in the Paris–Dakar Rally.

483 • A buggy speeding through the sunset during the Tripoli-Ghadames leg of the 12th Paris–Dakar Rally.

484-485 ● A frequent sight during the Paris–Dakar Rally: an overturned Mitsubishi, observed by its unharmed crew.

485 ● A crew attempting to free its vehicle from the sand during the 1985 Paris–Dakar Rally.

486 • Not many cars engaged in the Dakar Rally look like road models, but are closer to dune buggies in appearance.

487 • The Ford Raid X.202 built for the Dakar Rally has a Kevlar body and a 4000 cc V8 engine capable of generating 270 hp.

● One of the stars of the Dakar Rally, Mitsubishi achieved its fifth consecutive victory in 2005, the tenth since it started participating in the event.

Argentina

- This Ford Focus RS
lands badly during the
2000 Rally Argentina.

492 • A great leap into the water fully hides this four-wheel-drive Subaru Impreza, photographed during the 2005 Rally Argentina.

493 • A Peugeot 307 almost gliding over the ground in the 2005 Rally Argentina.

494 • A Subaru Impreza with its wheels almost entirely off the ground during the 2005 Rally Argentina.

495 • A mud-spattered Ford Focus fording a river in the rain during the 2000 Rally Argentina.

Monte Carlo

496-497 • A Lancia Delta engaged in a scenic mountain stretch of the 1986 Monte Carlo Rally.

497 • An aerial view of a Ford Focus tackling the winding mountain course of the 2005 Monte Carlo Rally.

498-499 ● A Citroën Xsara entering a turn during the 2005 Monte Carlo Rally.

499 ● The spectacular uphill stretch of the 2005 Monte Carlo Rally that leads to Col de Turini.

500-501 ● A Citroën Xsara climbing a mountainside during the 2005 Monte Carlo Rally.

501 ● Another Citroen Xsara, this time in red livery, in the 2005 Monte Carlo Rally.

502 • The 1994 Monte Carlo Rally also featured snow, tackled here by a Ford Escort RS Cosworth

503 • A Peugeot 306 Maxi with a damaged nose following a jump during the 1998 Monte Carlo Rally.

Corsica

A Peugeot 206 Super 1600 about to roll over during the Tour de Corse.

Sardinia

506 • A Subaru Impreza fording a river during the 2005 Rally Italia–Sardinia.

507 • The Japanese Subaru Impreza again, this time in the air during the 2005 Rally Italia–Sardinia.

508 • Citroën's smallest car, the C2 – shown here in the Super version – also participated in the 2005 Rally Italia–Sardinia.

509 • A Mitsubishi Lancer rounding a turn on the dirt terrain of the 2005 Rally Italia–Sardinia.

RACES

INTRODUCTION Track Races

Whwn speed is in the limelight, racetracks are the quintessential stages. Racing is a spectacle that excites our innate spirit of competition. This instinct allows us to discover and exceed our limits through competition and is at the center of each challenge, four-wheeled or otherwise. The car is one of those inventions that has changed the course of history and was quickly adopted as a means for challenging, competing, and winning – initially on roads and, as these got busier, on tracks closed to traffic. Indeed, the racetrack allowed speed to be expressed more freely and safely, while at the same time accommodating the public. The names of the temples of

INTRODUCTION Track Races

RACING – MONZA, INDIANAPOLIS, SILVERSTONE, DAYTONA, NÜRBURGRING, SPA-FRANCORCHAMPS, LE MANS, SEBRING, AND LAGUNA SECA – ARE CAPABLE OF CONVEYING INCREDIBLE EMOTIONS.

THE FIRST RACES TO BE STAGED ON CLOSED CIRCUITS WERE HELD IN AMERICA. THE UNITED STATES UNSEATED FRANCE, THE CRADLE OF THE FIRST ROAD RACES, WHEN A RICH YOUNG NEW YORKER BELONGING TO THE VANDERBILT FAMILY COMMISSIONED A CUP FROM THE JEWELER TIFFANY, WHICH HE OFFERED AS A PRIZE AT THE LONG ISLAND RACETRACK IN 1904. TRACKS HAVE SINCE BECOME THE PREFERRED STAGE OF FORMULA ONE RACING, THE STAR ON THE WORLD SCENE DEDICATED TO FOUR-WHEELED SPORTING EVENTS, WITH 2.9 BILLION

Track Races

SPECTATORS IN 200 COUNTRIES AND 70 HOURS OF LIVE TELEVISION EACH SEASON. IT IS THE JEWEL IN THE CROWN OF AN ARRAY OF RACES, WHICH ALSO INCLUDE SPORTS PROTOTYPE, TOURISM, GT, AND – IN THE UNITED STATES – CART, NASCAR, AND INDY CHAMPIONSHIPS, IN WHICH OVER 200,000 DRIVERS PARTICIPATE. RACETRACKS HAVE ALSO BEEN THE BACKDROPS FOR THE SPEED LEGENDS OF ALL TIMES: ASCARI, FANGIO, ICKX, STEWART, LAUDA, VILLENEUVE, AND SCHUMACHER; OR LOTUS, MCLAREN, FERRARI, AND TYRRELL – NAMES THAT HAVE EMBODIED COURAGE AND HEROISM, BUT ALSO TECHNOLOGY, PER-FECTION, AND PROGRESS.

- Racing is not just Formula One: a pit stop on the Talladega circuit for the 2005 NASCAR Championship.

Formula 1

516-517 •
A parade of spoilers
illustrating the array of
sponsors of
the Formula One
racing cars.

518-519 • Cars on
the starting grid at
the 1999 San Marino
Grand Prix, held at
the Imola racetrack.

520-521 • Team
companions Button and
Sato in the first turn
following the start of
the 2004 Monaco
Grand Prix.

Rubens Barrichello aboard his Ferrari on the starting grid of the 2001 French Grand Prix.

524 • A battle between the two Renault drivers Fisichella and Alonso during the
2005 Spanish Grand Prix.

525 • Alonso's Renault during a pit stop at the 2005 Brazilian Grand Prix.

526-527 • Jarno Trulli during his first season with Toyota at the 2005 Spanish Grand Prix.

527 • Montoya overtaking Schumacher before the chicane at the 2002 Brazilian Grand Prix.

528 • A crowded pit stop for Ferrari at the 1997 Brazilian Grand Prix.

529 • The curbs always create sparks, especially when the cars are traveling at very high speeds, like Eddie Irvine aboard his Ferrari at the 1998 Belgian Grand Prix.

530-531 • Braking at the first chicane immediately after the start of the 1998 Canadian Grand Prix .

532-533 • Giancarlo Fisichella aboard the Jordan-Peugeot during the 1997 Italian Grand Prix.

TOTAL
E
s.Oliver
EXCALIBUR
GdeZ
BENSON & HEDGES
GdeZ
MasterCard
BENSON & HEDGES
B&H
Diavia
GOODYEAR
FERRERO

534-535 • The brakes of Moreno's car glow white hot as he negotiates a turn during the 1991 Portuguese Grand Prix.

536-537 • The Ferrari and an airborne Williams were involved in a spectacular accident during the 2002 Australian Grand Prix.

● Alonso's Renault crashes into the wall at the 2004 Grand Prix in Indianapolis.

540-541 ● Herbert, off-track, shelters from a shower of gravel raised by another car at the 1998 Canadian Grand Prix.

542-543 ● Another Grand Prix, another foray into the gravel – this time by Giancarlo Fisichella at Monza in 1999.

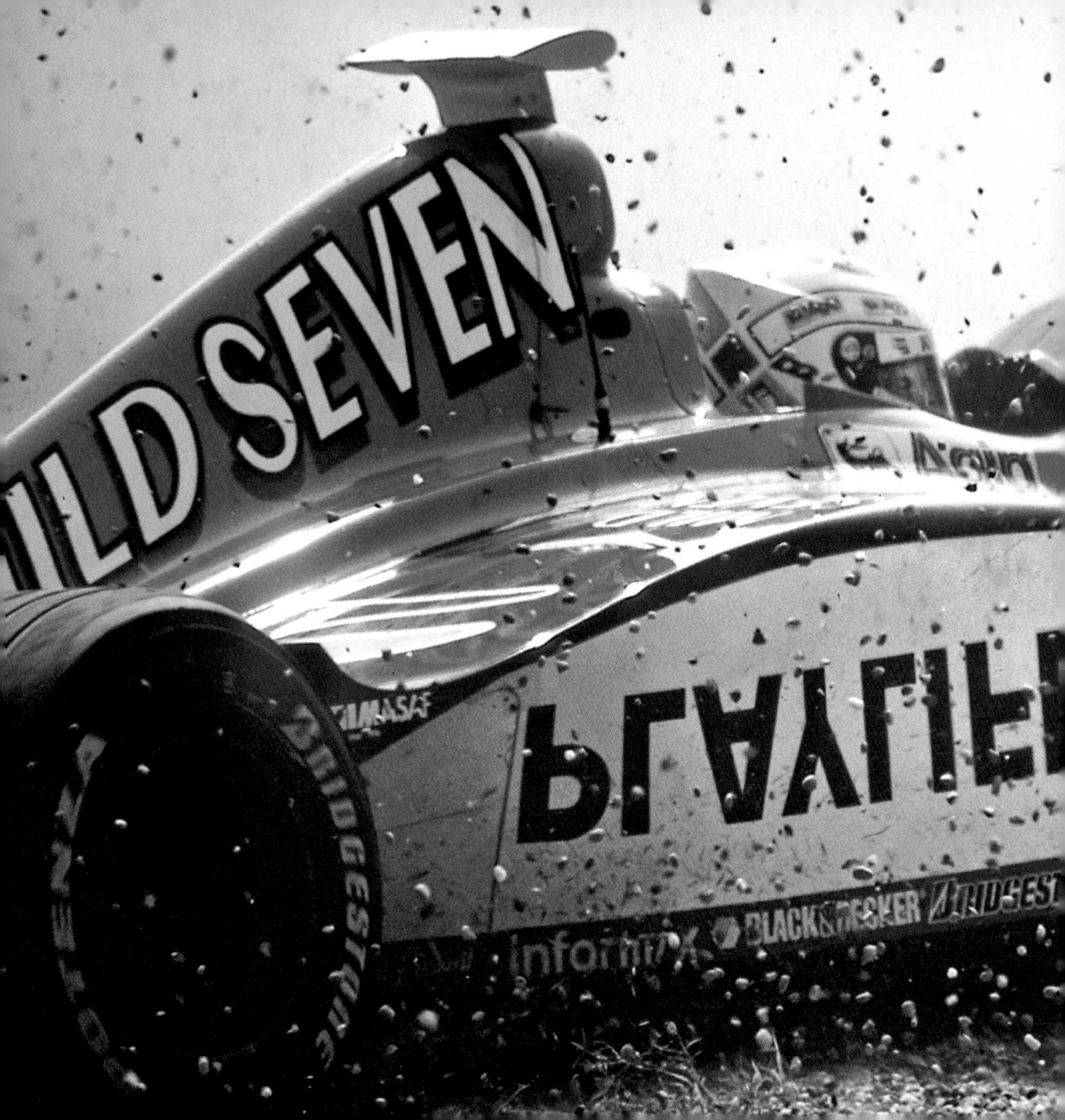
ILD SEVEN
BRIDGESTONE

A tire change and refueling during a pit stop at the 2002 Brazilian Grand Prix.

Eddie Irvine speeds away following a pit stop during the 2001 Spanish Grand Prix.

A close-up of Rubens Barrichello's single-seater at the 1999 Austrian Grand Prix.

A car takes to the air after hitting a Ferrari at the 2002 Australian Grand Prix.

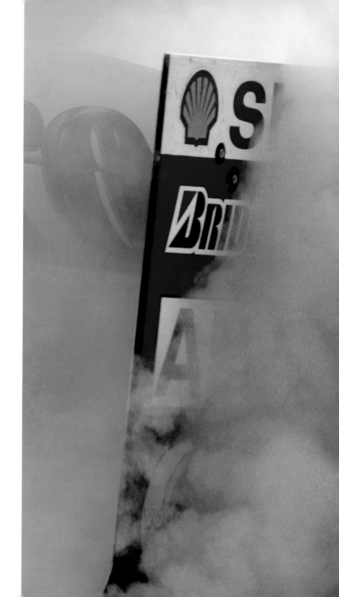

A flying start with smoking wheels for Schumacher at the 2004 Malaysian Grand Prix.

554 • A solitary Michael Schumacher cutting the finishing line of the 2001 Australian Grand Prix.

554-555 • A victorious Michael Schumacher passing the pits to celebrate his win in Australia in 2000 with the team.

556-557 • An evocative aerial view of Michael Schumacher's car during the 1999 San Marino Grand Prix.

Nascar

558-559 and 559 • Refueling during the 2005 NASCAR Championship: Indianapolis, left, and Michigan, right.

560-561 • A Chevrolet Montecarlo in the parabolic curve of the Lowe's Motor Speedway in Concord during the 2005 NASCAR Championship.

562-563 • An accident at Lowe's Motor Speedway in Concord during the 2005 NASCAR Championship.

563 • A spinning crash against the wall at Lowe's Motor Speedway in Concord during the 2005 NASCAR Championship.

564-565 • A spectacular collision between two cars during the Talladega race of the 2005 NASCAR Championship.

A Team Lowe's Chevrolet Montecarlo during a pit stop in the 2003 NASCAR Championship.

568 • The end of a hectic pit stop during a NASCAR race in Texas.

568-569 • An exciting pit stop during the Mountain Dew Southern 500 race of the 2005 NASCAR Championship.

570 • Sparks following contact with the wall of the parabolic curve at Bristol during the 2005 NASCAR Championship.

571 • Cars tackling the parabolic curve of the Bristol track during the 2005 NASCAR Championship.

572 • Smoke and spins during a Texas race of the 2005
NASCAR Championship.

573 • A collision with a wall during a 2005 NASCAR
Championship race in Dover.

Engine trouble following a crash during a 2005 NASCAR Championship race in New Hampshire.

Celebrations amid smoking tires for the winner of this race of the 2005 NASCAR Championship.

• Scenes of smoking tires, spins, and celebrations following one of the races of the 2003 NASCAR Championship.

Indy

580 • Cars speeding along the straight stretch of the Indy Japan 300 race of the 2005 IRL Championship.

581 • A moment during the pit stops of a 2004 IRL Championship race.

Entering a turn during an Indy Racing League race in St. Petersburg.

● Formula One–style single-
seaters competing in the
2005 (left) and 2004 (right)
Indy Championship.

A close-up of a Honda racing in the 2005 Indy Championship.

The pits are situated on the edge of the track in the Indy Championship, as can be seen in this photo taken during the 2005 season.

• Smoky moments during
a Japanese race of the 2005
IRL Championship.

The 2004 IRL Championship in the United States: a mechanic flings himself to the ground at the start of the race.

594 • A line of cars during one of the races of the 2004 IRL Championship.

594-595 • A pit stop watched by a large public during a 2004 IRL trial in the United States.

596 • A single-seater accelerates from a standstill during the 2004 Indianapolis race.

597 • A colorful car competing in the 2003 IRL Championship in the United States.

Le Mans

598 • A car passing beneath the Dunlop bridge during the 2000 Le Mans 24-Hour Race.

598-599 • Cars on the starting grid and a large public at the 1999 edition of the Le Mans 24-Hour Race.

600 • The sports prototypes await the start of one of the legendary races: the French Le Mans 24-Hour Race.

600-601 • This car in France's racing blue livery is playing at home in the 2002 Le Mans 24-Hour Race.

A BMW at dusk during the 1999 edition of the Le Mans 24-Hour Race.

604 • A Mercedes at night
during the 1999 edition of the
Le Mans 24-Hour Race.

604-605 • Toyota always wears
its red livery, even at Le Mans, as
shown by this car participating in
the 1999 edition of the race.

606 • The winner of the 2005
Le Mans 24-Hour Race: the Audi
R8 of the US Team Champion
Racing, driven by Lehto, Werner,
and Kristensen.

606-607 • British pride: the RML
team's Lola-MG, driven by Erdos,
Newton, and Hughes, which
finished in 21st position in the
2005 Le Mans 24-Hour Race.

CARS

This sporty and bizarrely colored Custom Frankenstude features an airplane-like nose.

INTRODUCTION Art Cars

Few of us can claim never to have heard someone say, "that car is a work of art." Although the statement is usually a cliché, the design perfection achieved by certain cars sometimes makes it a fitting description. Furthermore, many artists have appropriated and reinvented the appearance of the car, investigating its social role and its effects on the collective imagination, often giving rise to completely new forms.

Then there are those who have conceived the car as a canvas. BMW has established the Art Car Collection, close to its headquarters in Munich. This permanent exhibition features cars painted

INTRODUCTION Art Cars

BY FAMOUS ARTISTS, SUCH AS ROY LICHTENSTEIN, ANDY WARHOL, ERNST FUCHS, KEN DONE, A.R. PENCK, AND SANDRO CHIA. SINCE 1975 THESE MASTERS HAVE LENT THEIR BRUSHES TO CREATE AUTHENTIC FOUR-WHEELED MASTERPIECES. THE COLLECTION WAS THE BRAINCHILD OF FRENCH RACING DRIVER HERVÉ PULAIN, WHO ASKED THE AMERICAN ARTIST ALEXANDER CALDER TO PAINT HIS CAR FOR THE LE MANS 24-HOUR RACE. THE EX-TRAORDINARY COLLECTION HAS SINCE BEEN EXPANDED WITH THE WORK OF ARTISTS FROM ALL OVER THE WORLD. IN THE UNITED STATES THE CONCEPT OF THE ART CAR HAS ALSO BEEN EXPRESSED IN WHAT IS PER-HAPS A LESS NOBLE, BUT EQUALLY INTERESTING MAN-NER. FOLLOWING WORLD WAR II, MANY YOUNGSTERS

Art Cars

Introduction

RESTORED OLD CARS (FROM FORD MODEL TS TO 1920S AND '30S CHEVROLETS), DISMANTLING THE BODIES, LEAVING THE ENGINES EXPOSED, CUTTING AWAY THE ROOFS, AND ADDING WIDE WHEELS TO LOW-SLUNG CARS WORTHY OF THE RACETRACK. THE RESULT WAS CUSTOM FEVER, WHICH SEIZED THE ENTIRE UNITED STATES, STARTING WITH CALIFORNIA. THE CREATIVE INDIVIDUALITY OF SOME HOT-RODDERS, SUCH AS ED "BIG DADDY" ROTH WAS UNBOUNDED AND ROTH'S "BEATNIK BANDIT" AND "MYSTERION" BECAME LEGENDARY AND UNIVERSAL SYMBOLS OF SPEED AND CREATIVITY.

613 • Skull truck "Sculpture" by Julian Stock (left) and Billy Rainbow, made in New Orleans.

614-615 • The Blastolene Special Concept Race Car features a 1950s Formula One car body and exposed mechanics.

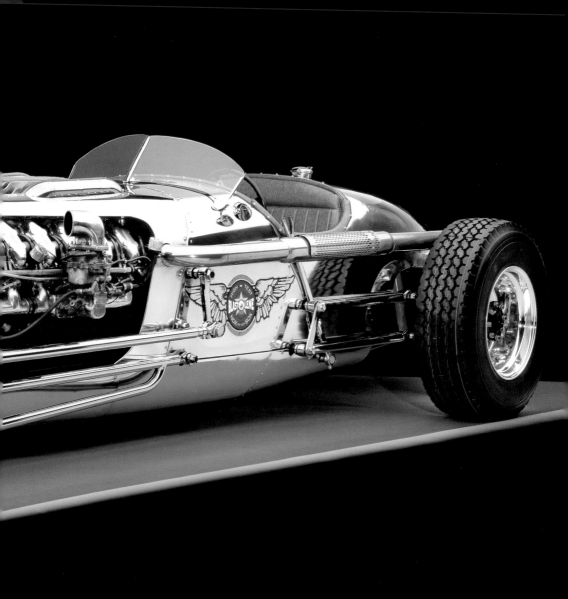

616-617 and 617 •
This fenderless 1932 Ford
Roadster Custom Convertible has
a long nose and a rounded tail.

618-619 • A side view of
the Custom Frankenstude:
note the pronounced shape
of the rear fenders.

620-621 • Another fenderless
model: the dragster-like
Aluma Coupe.

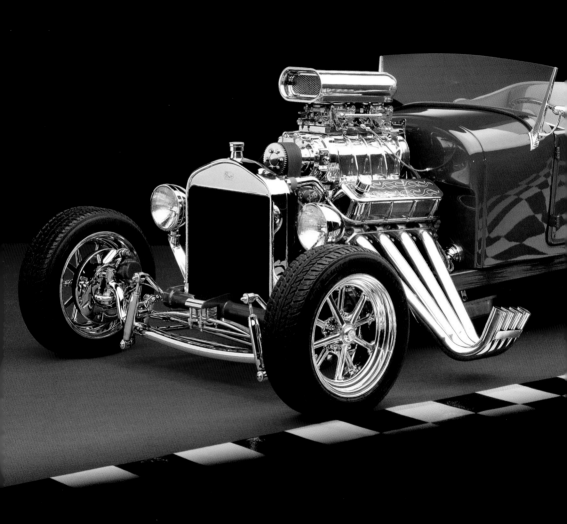

This dragster with exposed chrome engine is a reinterpretation of a 1927 Ford T Roadster.

624 • This 1932 Ford Hi Boy Roadster could easily have been the prototype for the cars in *The Fast and the Furious*.

625 • A detail of the free aspirated engine of the 1932 Ford Hi Boy Roadster.

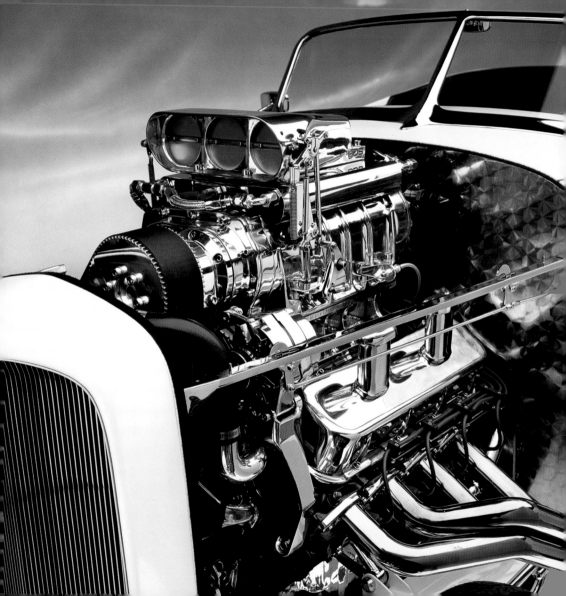

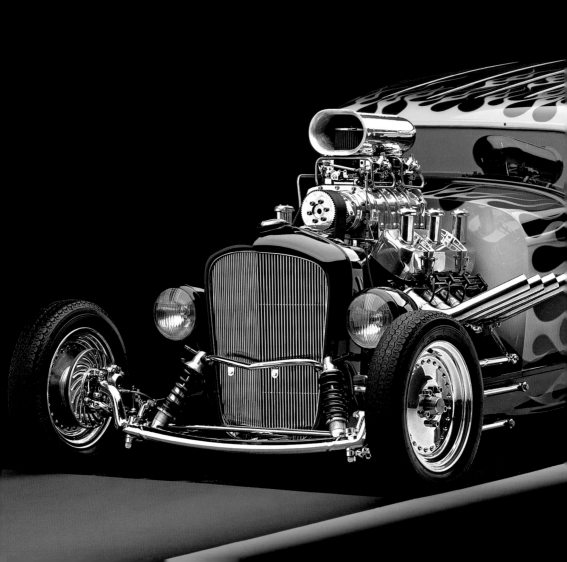

626-627 • Four-wheeled excess: note the giant rear wheels on this Ford Tudor.

628-629 • This 1933 Ford Plumb Crazy Street Rod features chromework and eye-catching running boards.

630-631 and 631 • The 1940 Ford Deluxe Opera Coupe is a low-slung muscle car with tiny lights set in the ribs.

632-633 • An alien is depicted on the tail of this 1934 Ford Custom Roadster, as announced by the vanity plate.

634-635 • This 1939 Ford Coupe boasts an unquestionably sporty flame-red livery.

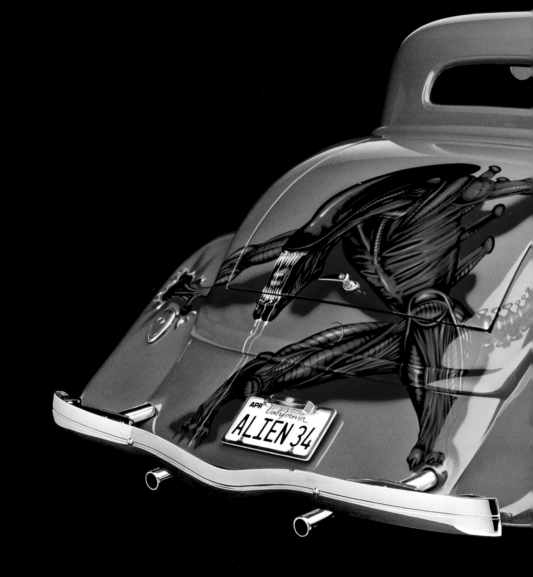

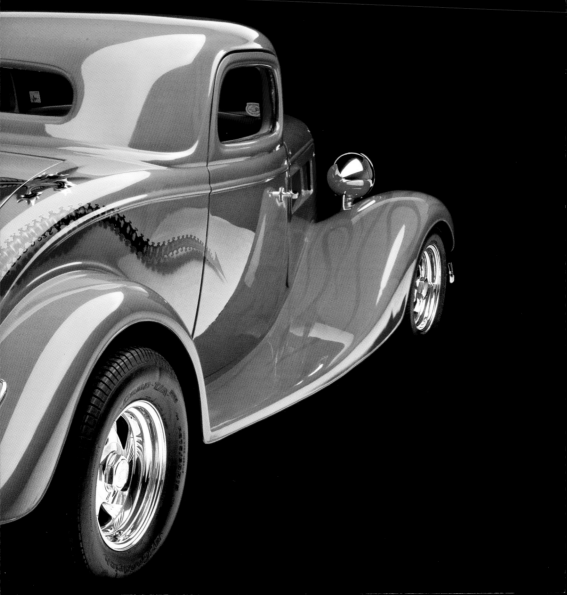

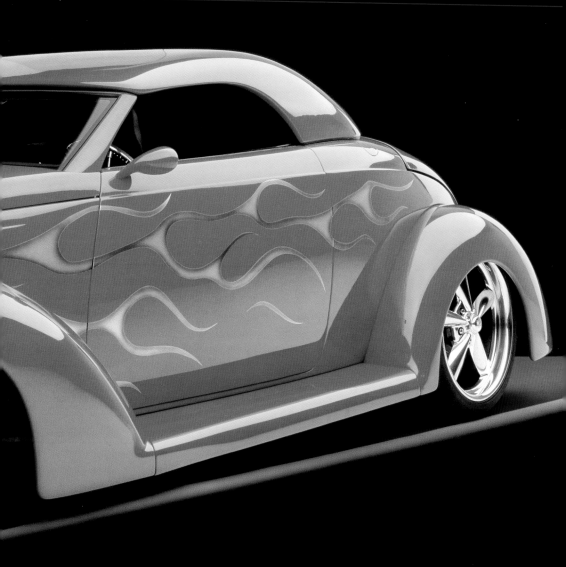

636 • This 1936 Ford Cole Foster 3 features an unpainted bare metal body and rear fenders.

637 • The 1936 Ford Cole Foster 3 is entirely metallic, except for the headlights.

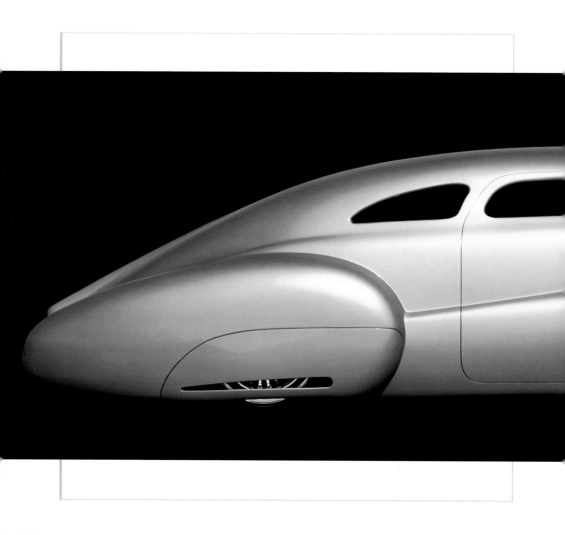

This 1948 Roadmaster Custom resembles a crouching bird when viewed from the side.

640 and 640-641 ● This 1949 Mercury Custom Street Rod is distinguished by the flames on its sides and built-in rear fenders.

642-643 ● The color and decorations of this 1950 Plymouth Deluxe Low Rider "Pura Vida" are very picturesque.

644-645 ● This 1951 Mercury 2-Door Convertible combines flames and fairing.

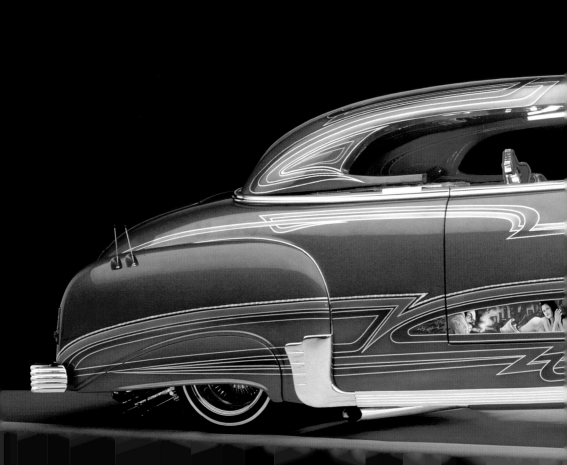

646-647 ● This highly original 1959 Cadillac Custom "Cadstar" is completed by fins.

648-649 ● This 1957 Ford Fairlane is almost identical to the mass-produced model.

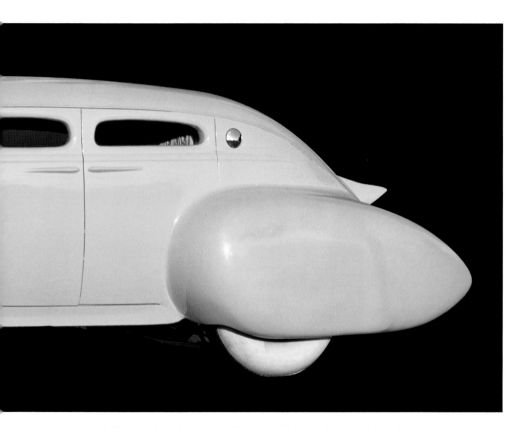

The design of this 2000 Gangster Custom Car is highly exaggerated, especially in the nose and fenders.

652 and 653 ● This retro-style fenderless Torpedo Roadster, built in 2002, features an eye-catching wing-shaped handle to open the trunk.

654-655 ● This customized Speed Star Coupe (2004) boasts blue flames.

656-657 ● The 1996 Elvis Presley Tribute features headlights like glasses and "custom" bumpers.

658-659 and 659 ● The 1941 Packard Convertible Custom Burgundy "Gable" is as refined as its name.

660-661 ● This 1959 Bentley S was customized for John Lennon.

662-663 • Music-loving Harrod Blank of Berkeley, California, has expressed his passion in his "Pico de Gallo" VW Beetle.

664-665 • Californian Larry Fuente's passion for ducks and swans is clear to see in his "Mad Cad."

666 • Larry Fuente's "Rex Rabbit"
(ArtCar Museum, Houston, Texas)
is a four-wheeled tribute to rabbits.

666-667 • "Eelvisa," by Shelley Buschur
of Houston, Texas, resembles
a playground train.

668-669 •
Californian Ron Snow
is very proud of his
eccentric "Coltmobile."

670-671 • Pickups are
not immune to four-
wheeled art, as shown
by "Yard Sale" by Cass
Flag of Atlanta.

The "Button Hearse" by Dalton Stevens of Bishopville, South Carolina, is a riot of colored buttons.

"Ripper the Friendly Shark," left, faces "Max the Daredevil Finmobile," both customized by Tom Kennedy of Houston, Texas.

676 • "The Telephone Car," by Howard Davis from Avon, Massachusetts, could hardly have had any other name.

677 • Dennis Clay of Houston, Texas, created this "Mirror Image" of his VW Beetle.

678-679 • Rick Worth of Key West, Florida, created this tribute to the Titanic.

CONCEPT
CARS

- In terms of design, practically anything goes for prototypes, as shown by this 2000 Buick Blackhawk.

INTRODUCTION Concept Cars

THE BASIS IS ALWAYS THE SAME: FOUR WHEELS RESTING ON A CHASSIS. SUBSEQUENTLY THE DESIGNERS WORK ON LINES, FORMS, AND NEW TECHNOLOGIES, GIVING FREE REIN TO THEIR IMAGINATIONS AND BUDGETS, DARING, TESTING, PROVOKING, EXPERIMENTING, AND CORRECTING UNTIL DEFINING A MODEL THAT MAY BE THE PREDECESSOR OF ANOTHER DESTINED FOR A LONG LIFE AND MILLIONS OF MASS-PRODUCED VEHICLES, OR A PROTOTYPE DESTINED TO WANE DURING THE BRIEF TIME SPAN OF A MOTOR SHOW.

CONCEPT CARS MUST CAPTURE THE ATTENTION OF THE PUBLIC AND REPRESENT A SAFE-CONDUCT FOR THE FUTURE OF THE BRAND. THEY ARE A SYMBOL OF ITS DESIGN, MECHANICAL, AND ELECTRONIC TRENDS, EX-

INTRODUCTION Concept Cars

PRESSED IN A SUBTLE GAME OF CLEAR AND OPAQUE, TENTATIVE NOSES, SOUPED-UP TAILS, AND FUTURISTIC DEVICES. PROTOTYPES ARE OFTEN THE WORK OF STYLISTS AND DESIGNERS, NOT JUST THE STYLE CENTERS OF THE MOTOR MANUFACTURERS. THE MODELS HAVE BIZARRE NAMES OR UNINTELLIGIBLE INITIALS, GO BY THE DEFINITION OF SHOW CARS OR CONCEPT CARS, AND FORESHADOW THE MASS-PRODUCED VEHICLES, ALTHOUGH THEY CONTINUE TO BE THE REAL TRAINING GROUND FOR CARMAKERS.

IT IS DIFFICULT NOT TO NOTICE THEM ON THEIR PLATFORMS BENEATH THE BLAZE OF LIGHTS AND IMPOSSIBLE TO PASS THEM BY, FOR THEY ENTICE WITH THEIR COLORS AND ATTRACT WITH THEIR SPOILERS AND

Concept Cars

Introduction

CHROMEWORK. THEY DISPLAY BREATHTAKING ENGINES, SUPERB ELECTRONICS, AND PASSENGER COMPART-MENTS THAT ARE THE PARADISE OF INTERIOR DESIGNERS (FOR IT IS HERE THAT THEY CAN FULLY EXPRESS THEIR CREATIVE FLAIR). ALL LOVERS OF BEAUTY AND AESTHETICS CAN ADMIRE THEIR DASHBOARDS, INSTRUMENTS, SEATS, AND COLORS, WHICH ARE WORTHY OF FUTURISTIC SPACESHIPS. HOWEVER, PROTOTYPES PLAY A VITALLY IMPORTANT ROLE FOR CAR MANUFACTURERS, AS THEY SERVE TO TEST THE APPROVAL OF THE PUBLIC, WHICH – ACCORDING TO THE LEVEL OF ENTHUSIASM OR INDIF-FERENCE DISPLAYED – DECREES THE DESTINY OF A CAR.

- An entirely chromed single-seater roadster for the third millennium: the 2001 Rinspeed Advantage R One.

R1 ONE

686 • This futuristic 1950s LeSabre is in no way inferior to the Batmobile.

687 • Whether a spaceship or a prototype, the styling of the Alfa Romeo Bat 7 (1953-1956) is simply breathtaking.

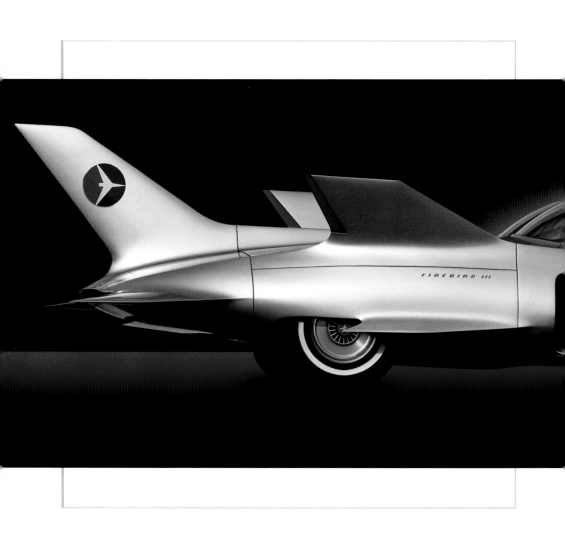

The design of this 1960s Pontiac Firebird III makes it resemble a four-wheeled fighter jet.

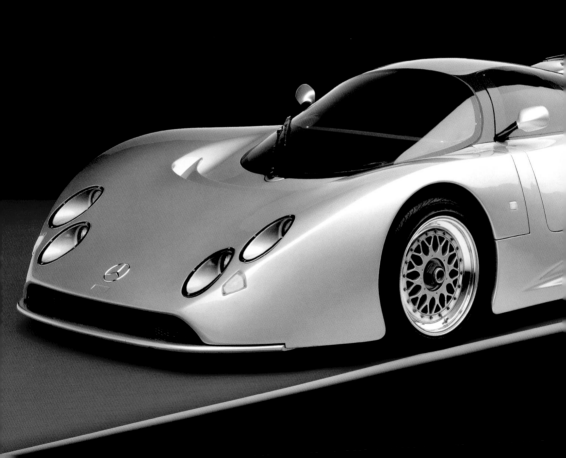

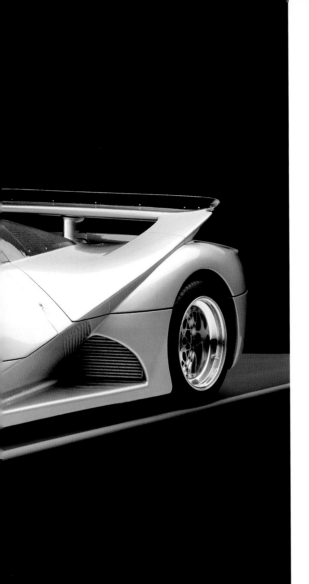

690-691 and 691 •
The Mercedes Lotec C1000 Silver,
presented in 1991, is clearly an
extreme GT car.

692-693 • Before becoming the
familiar hatchback seen on the
roads today, the Ford Focus was
presented as a concept car in 1992.

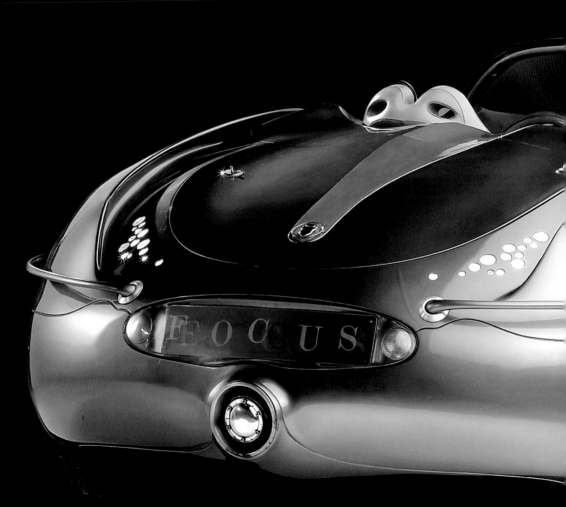

694-695 • The 1970 Lancia Concept car is shaped like a rocket.

696-697 • Elegant styling is the hallmark of the Chrysler Atlantic, created in 1995.

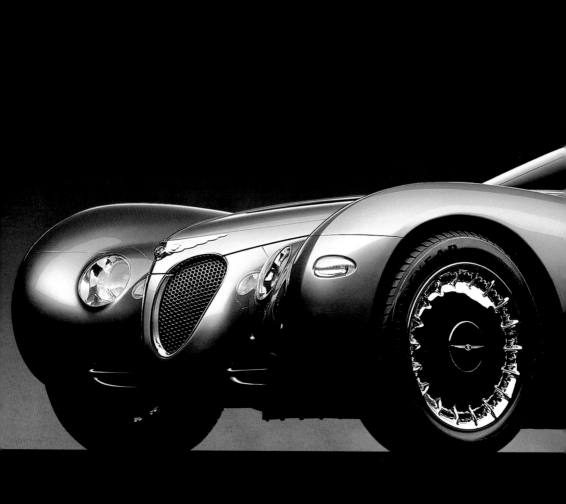

698-699 and 699 ● This Lamborghini Raptor Zagato, presented in 1997, features a targa body and large air vents.

700-701 ● The 1997 GT1 muscle car is unmistakably Porsche, particularly in the nose.

702-703 ● Only the shield betrays the origins of this Italian car: the Alfa Romeo Scighera, created in 1997.

704-705 ● This Le Blanc GT prototype, created in 1998, is largely unknown to the general public.

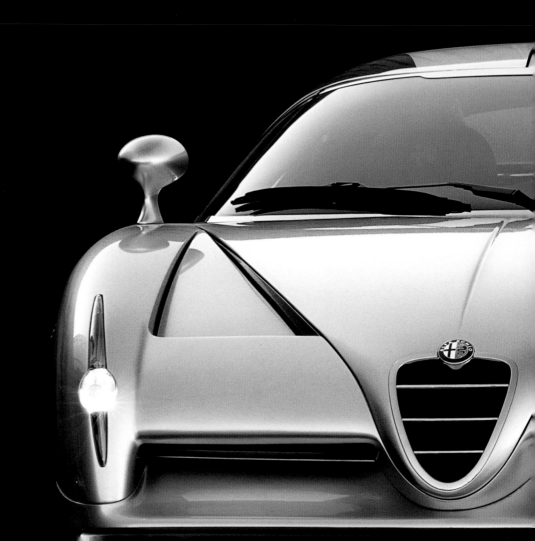

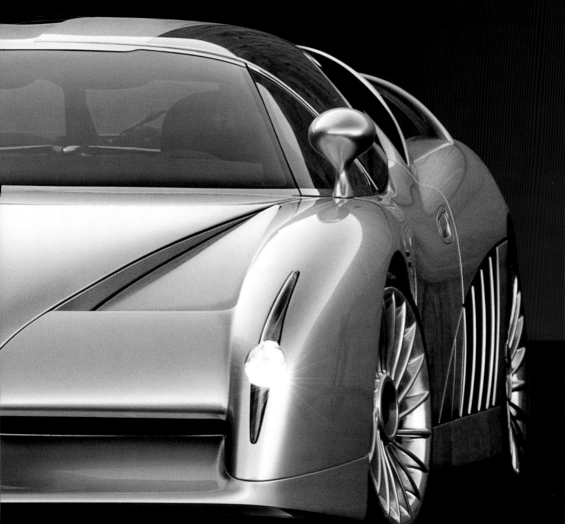

706-707 ● The appearance of the LE-1 Groundfighter fully lives up to the car's name.

708-709 ● The Buick Blackhawk, presented in 2000, is muscular even in cabriolet form.

710-711 ● The Rossa is a roadster in true Ferrari tradition, and was created to celebrate the year 2000.

712-713 ●
The highly original and unique tail of the Aviat Concept Car is a clear tribute to airplanes.

714 and 715 • This Spyker C8 Spyder T Silver Concept roadster is clad in silver livery.

716-717 • The name of the 2002 Venturi Fetish says it all.

718-719 • The 2005 Leaver GT Silver has a vaguely retro flavor.

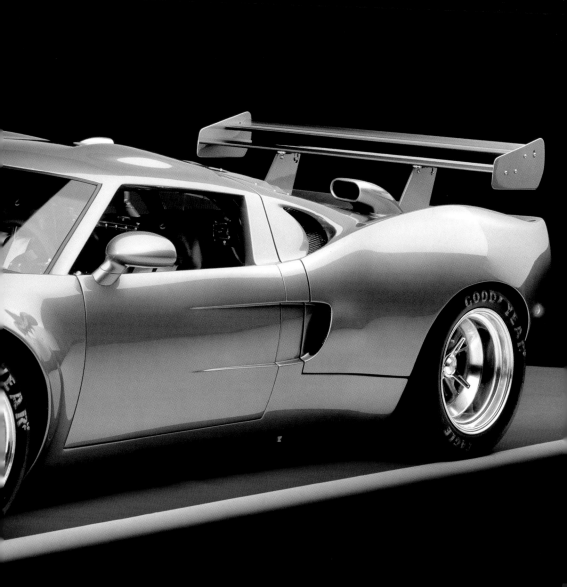

720-721 and 721 • A detail of the cooling grilles and angular spoiler of the Leaver GT Silver.

722-723 • The vital statistics of the Bugatti Veyron Black Coupe: 1001 hp, a 16-cylinder engine, and a top speed of 253 mph.

724-725 • The alluring road version of the Maserati MC12, created in 2005.

726-727 • This 2005 SSC Aero Copper resembles a mass-produced vehicle with sporting ambitions more than a concept car.

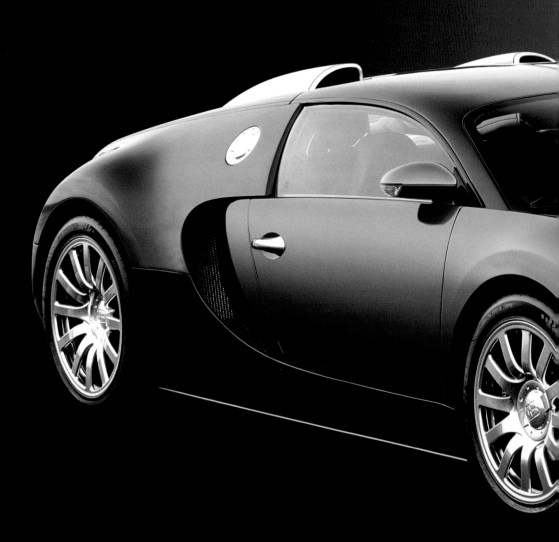

INDEX

PHOTO CREDITS

● The emblem of a 1931 Rolls-Royce Phantom I Regent.

Cover ● The 1997 Ferrari F50.

Back cover ● The 1957 Porsche Carrera Speedster Convertible.